Praise for the Lights...

"Scholars (Schlossberg, Waters, & Goodman, 1995) define transition as any event or non-event that results in changes in relationships, routines, assumptions, and roles. As it relates to sports, many athletes will face this difficult reality once their playing careers conclude. *Surviving the Lights* provides insights and strategies for athletes to employ to assist them as they exit the playing field to the next stage of life."

–Dr. Jamil Northcutt,
NFL Director of Football Administration

"Tywanna's book, *Surviving the Lights: A Professional Athlete's Playbook to Avoiding the Curse,* is spot on and is the perfect blueprint to assist and guide our young student-athletes through the most exciting, but pressure filled and stressful time in their lives. Awesome job, Tywanna!"

–Candy Murray,
Former Vice President of the Moms of Professional Basketball Players (MPBP) organization & Mom of Retired NBA player and current Lakers Assistant Coach Tracy Murray

"When I was drafted into the NBA, I had no idea what to expect. I wish I had this book in college. I am thankful to have had Tywanna as my business manager, but more importantly, as my friend."

–Sonny Weems,
Current NBA and Euro-League All-Star

"At the core of our mission in collegiate athletics is preparing student-athletes for the next phase in life. Tywanna's message focuses on the same values that we share with young people every day. Having a game plan to tackle the challenges in life is critical to forging a happy and healthy lifestyle."

–Kevin Anderson,
Athletic Director at The University of Maryland

"NFL players, and other professional athletes, should always remember to remain humble and remember that the proper planning of funds, living a well, yet modest lifestyle, and organization of responsibilities will last much longer than splurging and spending aimlessly on things that fade away. Surviving the Lights takes a proactive approach to helping collegiate athletes and their families develop a plan to address those critical success areas."

–Terrance Metcalf,
7-year NFL Veteran and current assistant coach at Pearl River Community College

"As a former collegiate athlete, I wish I had a mentor and someone who could prepare me for the challenges that came with that privilege. Thanks to my friend, Tywanna, current and future college athletes can use this book as a guide to surviving issues that many collegiate and professional athletes face."

–Clarence Jones,
NBA, NFL, and NCAA custom clothier;
Owner of CJ Custom Clothier
(His NFL client won Best Dressed in the 2016 NFL Draft)

"*Surviving the Lights* is just what the sports world needs right now. It's an honest wake up call for professional and college athletes alike to understand the magnitude of the responsibilities that come along with being in the limelight. It serves as a guide to show them how to take ownership of their lives and their careers from start-to-finish and to create a legacy that will honor them and their family name for decades to come."

−Yolanda Moore,
Two-Time WNBA Champion & Author of *Sell Out! Rules for Finding Work You Love*

"In my 17 years as an NBA sports agent, I've seen a lot of guys make mistakes because they were unprepared to handle the business side of professional sports. I've known and worked with Tywanna for many years, and I applaud her efforts to educate and guide young athletes and their families."

−Roger Montgomery,
Sports Agent at RocNation

"I enjoyed a successful 15-year career in the NBA and Europe, and there aren't many people that understand what it takes to play that long and be able to retire on your own terms. I have watched Tywanna grow into one of the brightest minds in the sports business, and she is the perfect person to address these issues."

−Marcus Brown,
Retired NBA & Euro-League Legend, Murray State & Arkansas Sports Hall of Famer

Surviving the Lights: A Professional Athlete's Playbook to
Avoiding the Curse
by Tywanna Smith

Crescendo Publishing, LLC
300 Carlsbad Village Drive
Ste. 108A, #443
Carlsbad, California 92008-2999
GetPublished@CrescendoPublishing.com
1-877-575-8814

ISBN: 978-1-944177-65-2 (P)
ISBN: 978-1-944177-66-9 (E)

Printed in the United States of America
Cover design by Melody Hunter

10 9 8 7 6 5 4 3 2 1

SURVIVING

the

LIGHTS

A PROFESSIONAL ATHLETE'S PLAYBOOK
TO AVOIDING THE CURSE

TYWANNA SMITH

Premier Business Manager to Elite Athletes

A Message from the Author

Surviving the Lights is available at Amazon beginning March 1, 2017.

https://www.youtube.com/embed/5mZZJg6HSHs

To help you implement the strategies mentioned in this book and get the most value from the content, we have prepared the following bonus gift we know you will love:

The 360° Branding Kit

Branding for the Pros

The most important trait that determines the long-term success of any brand is consistency – whether you are an athlete, an entrepreneur, or a professional. We have created *The 360° Branding Kit* to give you a blueprint to brand yourself or your business. We have compiled proven tips and guidelines from some of the top branding professionals in the business. In this kit, you will learn:

- What branding is (and is not)
- Why branding is important
- What a 360° brand consists of
- What your personal 360° brand campaign looks like

Happy branding!

You can get instant access to these complimentary materials here:

http://survivingthelights.com/

Dedication

To my son, Tyson, who I hope will one day survive the lights.
Thank you, my beautiful soul, for giving my life purpose.

Surviving the Lights
A Professional Athlete's Playbook to Avoiding the Curse

Why I wrote this book ...

This book is the continuation of a serious and overdue conversation in the sports world. As a Black woman operating in a male-dominated sports industry, I have witnessed social, economic, and media disparity among several athletes, specifically Black athletes. As a mother to a Black son, I understand how this disparity will, one day, impact how my son sees himself, the goals he sets for himself, and the decisions he makes with his greatness. I decided to write this book to not only explore the mistakes that many NFL and NBA professional athletes make, but to give you and your family a game plan that will help you avoid making those same mistakes.

Sometimes your natural inclinations will lead you to repeat poor life decisions because no one ever replaces "what not to do" with "what to do" in a way you can understand. It is hard for experts to offer solutions and connect with you if they do not understand, firsthand, the pressures and obstacles that come with being a professional athlete, specifically a Black professional athlete.

Although I've made several references to Black professional athletes, these obstacles exist for all athletes. However, for the purpose of this playbook, we will focus on NFL and NBA athletes. There are differences in each game, but the obstacles that both leagues' players face are largely the same. I challenge you to do your part to change the negative stereotypes of the sports world and to prevent other athletes from fitting into a negative statistic.

My story is like many other athletes' stories, and you may relate to different parts of my upbringing. Growing up in

West Memphis, Arkansas, to blue-collar parents who made co-parenting look easy, I was always searching for ways to make the most of everything I did or received. I wanted to learn all that I could, and reading books became my favorite pastime. Through my love of reading, I found creative ways to travel the world and learn about things that I never dreamed I would experience. This love of reading and of learning helped me balance the athletic ability I inherited. Many athletes allow their sport to consume them, but my parents set a standard of balance for me that enabled me to make a smooth transition into my post-career passion.

Like so many other athletes, having a younger sibling forced me to develop leadership traits that translated onto the basketball court. The patience and compassion that I gained from helping and teaching my younger sister molded me into a person who connected well with others—peers and authority figures alike. I learned early on that relationships are all we have in this world, and there was no amount of money that could replace them.

My parents sacrificed so much to travel with me on school and AAU basketball trips, and seeing so many players who had no one to support them made me appreciate their love and support even more. All young, elite athletes want to know that someone truly cares for them and not just what they can do on the field or on the court. It is extremely important to build their self-esteem. Imagine what it feels like to look up to see your parents in the stands. When I tore my ACL during my junior year of high school, my parents didn't fret about my future because they knew their academic standards would carry me no matter what happened with my athletic career.

After signing a full scholarship to play collegiate basketball at The University of Mississippi, my true growth began. I learned so much from my teammates and coaches, who all had different perspectives and experiences. I didn't have to go through certain things when I could learn from the mistakes of others. My collegiate career was wrought with various knee-related injuries, but because I was prepared to succeed in life, not just on the court, my experience was no less rewarding. I earned my undergraduate degree in marketing, then went on to complete my master of business administration from my alma mater. It was then that I decided to embark on my professional basketball career—but not until I had achieved my academic goals FIRST.

My two-year professional career in Europe was full of rich experiences, and I formed lifelong relationships with people around the world. When I was offered a position to join Merrill Lynch as a financial advisor, I knew the time to retire my basketball shoes had come, and the Lord was leading me to touch other athletes' lives through business. For almost a decade, I have worked with over a dozen NBA, NFL, and international athletes. Because I observed so many neglected areas of an athlete's professional needs, I was led to create The Athlete's NeXus, A Sports Marketing & Business Management Group for professional athletes. My group is different from other management groups because we don't exploit athletes for revenue; we prepare them for life. Many athletes may feel that they don't need help navigating their careers, but the high number of athletes that experience trouble in retirement tells me otherwise. We believe that if you start strong, you will finish stronger.

I have a unique perspective about the sports world that only a small percentage of professionals can relate. Per the US Census Bureau, only 8 percent of all financial representatives are minorities and a smaller percentage are minority women. How many of those minority financial representatives do you think are also former professional athletes? Not many! I think it is important to know that there are professionals that look just like you and that have successfully completed your sports journey.

This book is designed to be an easy read to help aspiring professional athletes and their families avoid the curse that

3

comes with the professional sports culture. Although most of the content in this book is relatively straightforward, it is necessary to explore because many athletes still make these mistakes every day. To find solutions, you must understand why these issues continue to surface. There is so much that each of us can do, right now, to improve, to advance, and to change the stereotypes. When we know better, we should do better, and there is no time like the present!

Pre-Game Warm Up

How can this playbook help me?

On the court, on the field, and in life, the sports game is about numbers. Your career success is broken down into points scored, field-goal percentages, touchdowns, rushing yards, wins and losses. Then, several post-career statistics hang in the balance: Will you end up in the 60 percent of NBA players who are broke within five years of retirement? Or the 80 percent of NFL players who exhaust their savings only two years removed from the game? I want to prevent as many professional athletes as possible from fitting into those negative post-career numbers.

I also believe we can change some other "numbers" that are too often attached to professional athletes' names: I want to increase the number of functioning foundations and charities run by athletes. I want to decrease the number of child-support cases that plague athletes and the number of athletes that squander money in high-risk investments they do not understand. I want to increase the number of athletes that finish college and help them raise their credit scores. I want to make sure every professional athlete leaves life insurance and a will for their family. I want to be able to hold you accountable for your own growth and success!

Have you ever wondered why so many professional athletes end up broke? How they go from being multimillionaires to bankrupt debtors within a short period of time? How they hear the stories of other athletes' mistakes but end up making the same bad decisions? Well, I have wondered about those questions repeatedly over the last decade, and I'd like to offer some guidance on how you can avoid that curse. Most books focus on the problems—poor money management, poverty mindsets, dishonest professionals—but they do not offer tangible solutions. Athletes operate best with good coaching, guidance, and teaching, and they are most receptive when someone connects with a level of understanding, not criticism. I know I do.

For the last ten years, I have worked very closely with NBA, NFL, and international athletes in various capacities—as a financial representative, business manager, and sports agency marketing director. I have been on "all sides of the ball," and my experience, observations, and research have led me to the conclusion that athletes and their families need more honesty, guidance, and coaching when it comes to their preparation for the professional level. Instead of being expected to pick up on subtle tips and suggestions from unique situations, you need a blueprint.

It is my prayer that this book will serve as a guide to any aspiring professional athlete at the high school or collegiate level; to any rookie professional athlete; and to any parent, coach, or person able to influence a professional athlete's life decisions. It is designed to explore why athletes make certain decisions and to provide solutions to prevent and overcome each obstacle. Usually, when we read the stories of professional athletes and their failures, we read for entertainment rather than understanding. I urge you to read this book for guidance.

If more professional athletes became better role models, better businessmen, and better citizens, the next generation of athletes would have a better shot at surviving the lights.

Understanding the structure: This book uses several sports analogies to help athletes frame their obstacles and options. At the beginning of each chapter, the problem will be labeled "Scouting Report." In sports, a scouting report is used to break down the tendencies, strengths, and weaknesses of an opponent to gain a better understanding, as well as, an edge. At the end of each chapter, the solution will be labeled "Game Plan." In sports, the game plan is the strategy or course of action the athlete or team should take to reach their objective—to win.

As you study this playbook, I suggest you do so with pen and paper. I will ask you questions throughout that will engage your thinking, challenge your self-evaluation, and inspire your confidence in your ability to enact change. You will be encouraged to make lists and gather information that will help you. There is considerable research on the effectiveness of a written plan and goal setting, so these tools will be vital to the success of your planning. Together, we can change this conversation, and it starts right now with you.

Read on to learn why so many athletes fall victim to the same vices and how you can avoid the curse!

Chapter 1

Creating and Building Your Legacy

SCOUTING REPORT — How can I start building my legacy?

"To succeed, you need to find something to hold on to, something to motivate you, something to inspire you."

–Former NFL running back, Tony Dorsett

-1-

Most athletes are concerned only about their athletic achievements and not the mark they can leave on the world. One of the most important things you must understand about your sports journey is that it is bigger than you.

Every decision you make, on or off the court or field, affects someone else and becomes a part of how you are remembered.

Creating a legacy is an important way to make your talent, success, and lifework lasting and meaningful. Your legacy should entail more than your performance or the time you played. You are more than a ball player! The Oxford Dictionary defines "legacy" as something left or handed down by a predecessor. Any athlete can give money, but what makes your contribution different from another player's is your reputation, interests, passions, and commitment to something other than yourself. My company spends a great deal of time branding our clients by coordinating their off-season activities, like speaking engagements, summer camps, and charitable endeavors. These activities showcase who you are, rather than your affiliation with your team. The athletes that have the greatest lasting impact are those who understand that their sport is merely a platform they can use to touch lives and make a difference in their own way.

Because so many life lessons are imparted through sports, athletes are often used to influence a younger generation of sports fans. Winston Churchill once said, "The price of greatness is responsibility." It is not up to you to determine if you WANT to lead a group of people or not; it comes with the territory. The sports world touches so many other areas of society and the economy, and it is a powerful tool to bring enthusiasts from different walks of life together. Corporations pay billions of dollars annually to use you as a marketing tool, so why don't you use your power and influence to create your own narrative?

Many athletes fail to build their legacy for several reasons: (1) they want to, but they wait (procrastinate); (2) they want to, but they don't want to do what it takes (refuse to commit); or (3) they simply don't want to (refuse to take responsibility).

The irony is that you will be remembered for something—either someone else's opinion of you or your own.

Oftentimes, negative off-court and off-field circumstances will taint your professional brand and personal reputation, and even overshadow your stellar performance. Most of the public information about you is what someone else believes, writes, or says, so it is important that you make good decisions and deliberately build the legacy you desire. Fortunately, there are several tools you can use to communicate who you are outside your sport, what you believe in, and what you'd like to do with your influence. Many athletes use social media, political activism, community service events, camps, and public relations to build their individual legacies.

During the 2016 NFL preseason, the San Francisco 49ers' Colin Kaepernick created a political and media firestorm when he decided to kneel during the national anthem to protest police brutality against minorities. Despite not being in the active rotation, he was attacked by fans, the media, other NFL players, and even political leaders. However, his silent protest sparked a desire in individuals and young athletes across the country to explore the origins of the national anthem and its omitted stanzas. As the 2016-17 NFL season continued, many Little League, high school, and collegiate athletes followed his lead and kneeled during each pregame playing of the national anthem. Regardless of his on-field performance, Kaepernick has cemented his legacy as an athlete that led a movement for justice.

Another athlete who has taken the initiative to successfully build his own legacy is the NBA's LeBron James. Although James is arguably the best active basketball player in the world, many people dislike him for some of his professional decisions and the manner in which he made them. Nonetheless, James donates his time and a great deal of his money each year to send thousands of children to school and to support impoverished areas of his community. Regardless of how anyone feels about him personally, it is hard to dislike someone who uses their status to bring so much good to their fans and community. In addition to his talent and performance, he will always be remembered for his philanthropy, his leadership, and his commitment to touching as many lives as possible.

In contrast, several athletes have allowed personal issues to taint their public image and legacy. OJ Simpson is probably one of the most memorable players in the history of football. He won the Heisman Trophy in 1968 and went on to set several NFL records. He then became a broadcaster and actor before being accused of murdering his wife and her alleged lover. After being acquitted of those criminal charges, Simpson was involved in a variety of legal disputes, such as a civil suit, a substantial tax lien, and a 2007 armed robbery in Las Vegas of sports memorabilia. It is still hard to believe that one of the most decorated players in NFL history could make such terrible decisions in his personal life that would forever taint his legacy.

Remember, you are in control of your image, your brand, and your legacy.

Treat people kindly, speak up when it matters, and give as much as possible to help those in need. Your character will show in your interactions with others, so always do the right thing because it's the right thing to do. By incorporating these principles into your life, you will position yourself to be remembered positively long after you retire from your sport.

Ask yourself how you want to be remembered as a person, not just as an athlete. Imagine what you'd like people to say about you at your funeral. Make a list of those traits and the things you must do to be remembered that way. Most of your list should encompass how you treat and help others, not what you do for yourself. Start checking off your action items TODAY!

Chapter 2

Spotting the Leeches Before the Fame

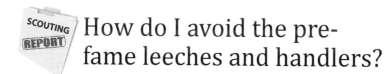 How do I avoid the pre-fame leeches and handlers?

"My biggest thing is I try to surround myself with good people and I try to keep my circle small."

–NBA forward, Thaddeus Young

-2-

Did you know that there are individuals that recruit players for the professional level before they are out of high school? These individuals are not necessarily agents, but they can be AAU coaches, Little League coaches, mentors, and even school personnel. While many of them have good intentions and genuinely want to help you grow into a well-rounded, successful athlete, a growing number of them try to get close to you for selfish reasons. It is not uncommon for these "handlers" to befriend your parents, relatives, or coaches for access to you.

You are building your legacy right now, and the people around you are a part of it.

The handlers strategically place themselves around you and your family as soon as you begin to rank high among your peers. The popular website Rivals.com is actually a network of websites that focuses mainly on football and basketball rankings. In 2015, players as young as sixth grade were included in its profiles. Rivals national analyst Mike Farrell said the site has no plans to rank players that young and that the youngest players to receive ratings will continue to be sophomores. Realistically, there is too much physical development left to accurately evaluate players in the sixth grade. However, it does bring recruiting into the conversation as colleges are increasingly offering scholarships to players as young as those in the eighth grade! This information is still important though, because it gives handlers a list to watch so that they know where to position themselves early in the process.

Player rankings introduce a new level of pressure that has financial undertones. Whether it is for scholarship money or for a professional contract, athletes and their families watch those lists religiously and judge their chances by their ranking. Handlers usually present themselves as someone with in-depth knowledge of the rankings system and high-level connections. Usually, they give you so much of their time, attention, and even money that you feel obligated to repay them for their investment in you. Some of these relationships are formed organically and transparently, but a great number of them happen strategically.

You will be forced to make a decision early
in your sports journey about what it will take
to make you compromise your standards.

Too many athletes choose money, and when they sell themselves to the highest bidder, that decision ultimately becomes their downfall.

Because several entities regulate sports agents and their contact with you and your family, sports agents must sometimes be creative when attempting to form an early relationship with you. Many agents have relationships with "runners" who are not bound by agent regulations because they are not licensed by the regulating authority. However, the agent will compensate the runner for gaining access to you, your family, or your handler and for their influence once you are able to sign a professional contract. Some of these runners are already on the sports circuit and can be a good guide for you, yet some are involved only to line their own pockets, gaining access to you to sell you to the highest bidder.

Sometimes, it is hard to spot the runner because they usually understand the football or basketball business, and oftentimes they are former professional athletes. They may offer to help train you, to introduce you to someone famous, or even to give you money for bills or clothes. In some cases, this person may even invite you or your family into their home by convincing your parents that playing for a certain school or team will improve your chances at a collegiate or professional opportunity.

The desperation that you and/or your family exhibit for financial relief will teach people how to treat you.

If the handlers and runners know that they can accomplish their goals by dangling money, gifts, or promises in front of you, then you have introduced a distraction to your greatness into the conversation. From that moment on, you will spend time thinking about what you can gain now versus what you should work to earn later. My advice is to be patient with the process. There is nothing worse than working your entire life for something, only to have it ripped from you because your past mistakes caught up to you. Remember, all your decisions and their consequences will become a part of your legacy, so choose wisely.

 Make a list of anyone that is close to you outside of your parents, and write down how you met them. Be cautious about any person that you didn't meet naturally and who seems too eager to help. If it seems too good to be true, it usually is. Even if you've accepted aggressive advances in the past, you can always politely decline their advances moving forward. Don't risk your future on short-term pleasure.

Chapter 3

Filling the Roles on Your Professional Team

 How do I build my own team of professionals and supporters?

> *"One man can be a crucial ingredient on a team, but one man cannot make a team."*
>
> –NBA legend, Kareem Abdul-Jabbar

-3-

While it is difficult to ascertain the motives of the people around you, as a professional athlete, you must seriously consider them as it pertains to your professional support team. Sports is big business, and because some professional athletes can have very lucrative careers, they run their lives like a business. Every athlete should contemplate what their professional team should look like. Whether you select a one-stop-shop sports agency that offers a variety of marketing and management services or hire your own personal team outside of your sports agency, make sure you are clear on everyone's qualifications and roles as well as any potential conflicts. Your team should make your life easier and help you grow along the way.

One of the first decisions you will make as a professional athlete is who will represent you. Try not to get caught up in the big names an agent represents because most mega-agents will try to name-drop athletes to convince you of what they can do for your career. You are not like any other player. Your game, your personality, and your strengths put you in a class by yourself. What an agent can accomplish for one athlete may not be a good fit for you. Focus, instead, on their ability to service YOUR unique needs and fulfill YOUR career goals. There are several benefits to working with a one-stop-shop sports agency. For instance, you can usually ensure that everyone is working together, and your overall fees are typically lower. However, the negative aspects of utilizing a one-stop-shop sports agency present a strong argument for professional athletes to have their own personal teams.

One of the biggest drawbacks to working with a one-stop-shop sports agency for services outside contract negotiation is the lack of personal attention each client receives. This has prompted more boutique agencies to pop up promising a higher level of personal attention to potential clients. The idea is that large sports agencies have multiple clients and do not have the time to service them all effectively. The top revenue-producing clients get all the agent's attention, leaving the rest to fend for themselves. Additionally, if the agent has his hand in too many of your dealings, that relationship could reveal a potential conflict of interest (a situation in which a person is involved in multiple interests, financial or otherwise, that could possibly corrupt their motives).

The NFL Denver Broncos' Russell Okung offers an interesting perspective about the player-agent relationship. He is quoted in a 2015 interview as saying, "The fact of the matter is that even if the agent-player relationship is a close, heartfelt, personal one, it's still founded on one thing: money." Okung ultimately decided to fire his agent and represent himself, negotiating his own multiyear deal with the Denver Broncos. He felt he shouldn't have to pay someone a fee to market himself, and the decision has paid off for him.

Whatever decision you make about the structure of your team, every business relationship needs a system of checks and balances.

If you have a system of checks and balances, that means someone else is there to ensure that every person on your team is doing what they are supposed to do, and that they are not taking advantage of you to serve their own interests. If the president of the United States operates under a system of checks and balances to ensure that one person does not become too powerful, exercise too much control, or face a conflict of interest, the same principle should be applied to your agency relationship. Too many athletes have suffered negative consequences because their personal feelings for their agent clouded their judgment.

On every sports or professional team, everyone plays a role. As long as each individual does what they do best and everyone works together, you should win.

Allowing people to operate where they are most qualified and where they have the most experience will ultimately benefit you. If everyone on your team has the common goal of helping you become more successful, you should not experience any conflicts, whether they are with the same company or not. Ultimately, you want to make sure all facets of your career get the attention they deserve, and there is nothing wrong with forming a well-rounded team. Athletes such as the NBA's Draymond Green, Carmelo Anthony, and Tristan Thompson have reaped the benefits of having a balanced, qualified team, as have the NFL's DeSean Jackson, Cam Newton, and Vince Young.

You will need to fill some common roles on your professional team. You will most likely need an agent. However, there has recently been much controversy among several players regarding the need for an agent due to the stipulations set forth in the collective bargaining agreements, the legally binding agreements between both the NFL and its players and the NBA and its players, that define the terms and conditions of player contracts. You will need a financial professional to assist you with your financial decisions, investments, and budgets; a marketing team to help you brand yourself, secure endorsements, and position you for revenue opportunities; and some athletes hire business managers or personal assistants to help them handle day-to-day nuisances and to care for their family in their absence. There are cost-effective ways to build your team, so take your time when choosing who will represent you. At a minimum, they should be experienced, trustworthy, and professional, and they should understand how to work with professional athletes. Many athletes experience problems in their business relationships because they don't take the time to vet those they work with from the beginning.

There are several ways to check a professional's licensing in the sports industry. NBA agents are certified through the National Basketball Players Association (NBPA), and NFL agents are certified through the National Football League Players Association (NFLPA). The NFLPA has a program that also certifies financial advisors based on their background screening, length of service, liability insurance coverage, and licensing. While the NBA doesn't yet have a program for its advisors, any financial representative's credentials can be checked online through FINRA's BrokerCheck program. Enter the advisor's name, and you can check their work history, licensing, and any complaints brought against them. The NFL's Darren McFadden recently sued his former longtime business manager, saying he misappropriated and mishandled money throughout his NFL career, including $3 million dollars lost in a bitcoin business venture. He filed the $15 million dollar lawsuit in 2016. His advisor was an old friend, and at the time that the suit was filed, he had not been licensed by the NFLPA's advisor program or a financial firm for over five years! Do your homework on your professionals, and recheck them often.

Now, there are times when agents get criticized for things outside their job description. Technically, their core service is contract negotiation and career guidance. Most agents include pre-draft preparation in their model because, obviously, if they can boost your draft pick and the guaranteed money associated with it, then they can boost their payday. Because most agents form such close relationships with their clients, they are oftentimes called upon to handle day-to-day affairs, such as making travel accommodations, handling legal affairs, and even counseling family members. While agents understand these activities are part of the relationship, most of them would rather not spend a great amount of time in things that will not produce income for them. Some activities are important to protect their investment in you, but they would rather not spend valuable time handling minute issues due to your immaturity, irresponsibility, or laziness. Their time is valuable because time is money.

Your sports agency will most likely have a person or department devoted to handling your marketing for income opportunities, such as endorsements, speaking engagements, and appearances. Their motivation is the same: when they earn income for you, they make money, too. Commissions on marketing deals range from 10 to 20 percent. After working as the director of marketing in a sports agency, I can tell you that if this is who handles your marketing, you will most likely miss out on some of your biggest needs, such as personal skills development, legacy building, and true post-career planning. The focus will be solely on maximizing your contract and revenue opportunities while you are actively playing, which is why I believe that athletes should have a separate marketing team to work with their agency team. One focuses on right-now income; the other focuses on developing your long-term brand and income-producing skill set.

I created my company, The Athlete's Nexus, to address the fundamental needs of athletes from several perspectives: marketing, business management, and personal development. It takes more than one person to manage an athlete's life. To date, there hasn't been much focus on developing an athlete's personal skill set, so I decided to create a model that would invest in the most overlooked areas of an athlete's life to prepare them to take advantage of the opportunities presented to them—now and into retirement.

Because so many professional athletes have trouble determining who they can trust, they sometimes hire family and friends as their business and marketing representatives. As a general rule, you should not mix business and personal relationships because they rarely end well. While these people are individuals you can trust, they usually do not have the experience, qualifications, or connections to help you maximize your short playing window. They become an extension of you, and several athletes have had their reputations tarnished due to the actions of their family and friends. You will fare best if you allow your parents to be parents, friends to be friends, and business professionals to be your business representatives. To compromise, many athletes allow their family members to perform very basic duties, such as house sitting, paying bills, and arranging deliveries. If you allow family and friends to work for you, make sure their payment is consistent with what someone with their skills, education, and experience is worth.

Lastly, I believe all professional athletes should have a mentor that has played their sport. There is a level of wisdom that can only come from walking in the same shoes. Your mentor should be someone whom you can call not only for advice, but someone who will warn you of potential conflicts and who is not afraid to tell you when you are on the wrong path. I pair each of my clients with a retired athlete from their sport. You will welcome an unbiased voice that understands the pressures of being in your position, and their experience is invaluable.

 Don't let your overconfidence in your ability to work with certain people cost you your family, your career, and your future. Don't be too trusting with one individual, no matter how well you get along. Leave the business to the professionals. Make a list of the qualified professionals in your family and close circle. Include at least one professional mentor that you have not yet met, but to whom you need to introduce yourself. Review your team often to make sure every member is accommodating your needs, and do not be afraid to make the necessary adjustments.

Chapter 4

Dealing with Family Members

How can I avoid ruining my family relationships?

"I played basketball to try to get my parents from working so hard."
–NBA Hall of Famer, James Worthy

-4-

For generations, the African American culture has instilled a "loyalty" complex in its offspring to make decisions based on emotion rather than logic. We are expected to support and help our family members and close friends when we get ahead, even if they do not want to help themselves. Many times, you will feel guilty about wanting to work with more qualified professionals because you don't want to "sell out." That self-imposed guilt has cost a great number of athletes a lot of money, a lot of opportunities, and a lot of relationships. Sometimes your most poisonous relationships will be with your family and friends, so prepare yourself to make some tough decisions.

When you consider why so many athletes experience financial hardship in retirement, you must reflect on how their introduction to money shaped their perceptions. The athletes in the NBA and NFL are predominantly Black. It is estimated that nearly 70 percent of NFL athletes and nearly 80 percent of NBA athletes are Black. It can be argued that most of these Black athletes were raised in single-parent homes and were subjected to various levels of poverty. When these athletes speak publicly about their upbringing, they usually comment on the struggle they witnessed their parent endure to care for multiple children, pay bills, and keep food on the table.

This memory sets the tone for the emotional pressure that money brings to your relationships with your family. Money is viewed as the answer to so many problems, many that have nothing to do with money. It is put on a pedestal as the rescue from a dire situation, and family members will anxiously await their cut of your first check to solve all their problems.

Many athletes will see their own worth in dollars and cents.

As you climb the success ladder, your commitments to everyone in your circle will begin to weigh on you. Regardless, your fear of hurting or disappointing your closest relatives will force you to continue to throw money at a situation you wish you could fully escape.

Most parents fail to realize the role they play in their child's future beliefs and decisions about money—however unintentional that role might be. What is important to your parents will become important to you. When your parents tell you that you can't play for a certain team because they can't afford it, or that they are stressed from not having enough money, you will begin to crave what you don't have, see power in it, and overlook a lot of the good you do have. Parents must take responsibility for their role in teaching young children that money is the answer. To combat this tendency, focus holidays and life events around the intangible gifts of love, quality time, compassion, and hand-made gifts. If you choose to exchange gifts, make sure they have a dollar limit.

For most professional athletes, this toxic money mentality happens over a period of time, and before you know it, you're sending money for all holidays and special occasions. After a while, money will replace the time you spend together, and you will depend on money, instead of love, as the foundation of your relationship. This is the trap that ruins relationships. All at once, you seem to convince yourself that no one can survive without the money you give them, and you justify the habit you have created. You don't realize that your largely self-imposed mental and financial ruin has taken root.

One athlete that has solid advice on how to deal with friends and family is the NBA's Kobe Bryant. In a letter to his younger self that he wrote as an editorial for *The Players'*

Tribune, Bryant imparts the following nuggets of advice from his personal successes and failures:

"You need to figure out a way to invest in the future of your family and friends," Bryant wrote. "I said INVEST. I did not say GIVE."

"You will come to understand that you were taking care of them because it made YOU feel good," Bryant wrote. "It made YOU happy to see them smiling and without a care in the world—and that was extremely selfish of you."

"Trust me," Bryant wrote, "setting things up right from the beginning will avoid a ton of tears and heartache."

Bryant has had a rocky relationship with his family. He has not spoken to his parents for several years, following a dispute about money. His mother was not pleased with the size of the home he offered to buy her and wanted something larger and more extravagant. She then auctioned off valuable pieces of his sports memorabilia, including his old jerseys, championship rings, and trophies. She netted a $450,000 advance on the items that were worth over $1.5 million, with plans to purchase a larger home in Nevada. Kobe battled legal issues with his parents and the auction house to recover the items as his parents did not have permission to sell the collectibles. He eventually settled with the auction house for an undisclosed amount to retrieve his memorabilia.

The NFL Dallas Cowboys Tyron Smith was completely overwhelmed by his family's requests for money. Smith had agreed to buy his parents a home for $300,000, only to find the home they wanted was priced north of $800,000. Over the course of a year, Smith ended up shelling out over $1 million to his family. When he received news of a promotion and a larger contract after his rookie year, his family's reaction wasn't to congratulate him but to ask him the amount of his contract. Situations like this happen frequently and usually mark the beginning of an athlete's erosion of trust and control. If your closest family members want you only for money, it becomes hard to determine whom you can trust. At the same time, you feel guilty for wanting to say no, so you let your parents have their way. This is the reason so many relationships break down.

Former NFL player Phillip Buchanon was a first-round NFL draft pick and played nine seasons in the NFL. He recently released his first book, *New Money: Staying Rich*, to give his account of what it's like to be a professional athlete. In his own experience, his newfound wealth dramatically changed his relationship with his mother. Once drafted, Buchanon's mother told him he owed her $1 million for raising him for the past eighteen years.

Imagine your mother saying those things to you during one of the most important moments of your life! Instead of supporting you and celebrating your success, the focus immediately goes to what you can do for everyone else. These conversations harden something within an athlete and cause them to be cautious, even with those with the purest of motives.

My advice is to never send your parents, family members, or friends monetary gifts for recurring occasions like birthdays, anniversaries, and holidays. Money becomes the standard, and once you start, everyone expects the amount to increase. If you must purchase gifts for them, know that the most thoughtful gifts are not always the most expensive. Give more of yourself and your time, reminding yourself that at one point, that is all you had to give. If you start with this advice, you won't have to damage a relationship when you are no longer able to finance it. Moreover, your bond will always remain pure. It is a good idea to have the conversation before becoming a professional athlete so that all expectations are clear. Many times, athletes assume these situations will never happen to them because they were never addressed directly.

 It is never too late to make better decisions! Learn to share ideas and experiences instead of dollars and cents. When you change your mind-set, your relationships will change, but they will be more valuable. Create connections that will remain the same when money is removed from the conversation. Create a calendar of events for the next twelve months that includes quality family experiences without a financial focus. Make sure you have someone in place that can say "NO" for you to your closest family members and friends.

Chapter 5

Addressing Mental Health Issues in Professional Sports

 How can I protect my mental health?

"Difficulties in life are intended to make us better, not bitter."

–NFL Veteran & Coach, Dan Reeves

-5-

Money, family, and even career issues can affect you mentally, and the topic of mental health in professional sports has gotten more attention over the past few years in the NBA, NFL, and abroad. Several top athletes have earned their rise to stardom by learning how to productively channel their mental health struggle on the court or field. Their on-field and on-court success masks symptoms of the problem until a traumatic event unleashes the illness. According to an Australian sports medicine study, leading experts suggest that nearly 50 percent of elite athletes suffer symptoms from at least one mental health problem, such as depression, psychological distress, or anxiety.

I would venture to say that the number could be higher by adding other illnesses, such as addiction, bipolar, and phobia disorders.

Mental health is often overlooked and sometimes dismissed in society, in sports, and especially in the Black community. The negative stigma associated with the topic prevents many athletes from admitting that they exhibit symptoms of mental illness and from seeking help. Most men are not likely to seek help, and Black men are even less likely. Sadly, they force themselves to suffer in silence because they fear that others won't understand or help them work through their issues. This illness can plague you as a youth, as an active player, and well into your post-career.

Much of the debate about mental illness in sports addresses the league's support for its players. NBA teams conduct various psychological evaluations and interviews during their pre-draft and post-draft assessments. They use these evaluations to measure an athlete's general mental health, their ability to fit the team dynamic, and their overall readiness for the professional level. Because mental illness is an illness of the mind, many symptoms can go undetected. However, if it is decided that an athlete is mentally healthy enough to function, there is no support to help the athlete cope with any underlying illness. NBA players suffer from a number of mental health issues, most often depression and anxiety. NBA teams do not have mental health professionals to work with their players, and confidentiality becomes a huge issue when medical professionals outside the league address the illness.

In addition to the mental stress of professional sports, NFL players have a higher risk of experiencing mental illness due to physical injuries, such as post-concussion syndrome or chronic traumatic encephalopathy (CTE). CTE is a progressive degenerative disease affecting people who have had repeated blows to the head, such as the concussions that plague NFL players. Physical injuries can severely impact an athlete's quality of life as short playing careers translate into long lives full of pain. While the NFL has attempted to protect itself financially from post-career lawsuits through various education tools, much still needs to be done to diagnose, treat, and protect its athletes from the negative consequences of untreated mental illness.

There are certain circumstances that put you at higher risk for mental health disorders, such as poverty, family dynamics, injuries, and career failures. In some cases, bouts of illness can come and go during stressful times, like team trades, waivers, firings, and career-ending injuries. Stress and physical trauma have even pushed some athletes to commit suicide. Did you know that mental illness can also be genetic—that it can be passed down through families? In a world that stresses mental toughness, it becomes hard for an athlete to determine what is normal and when to seek help.

Mental illness episodes can be triggered by several issues, such as public scrutiny, injury, career disappointments, and unpreparedness for retirement. Several athletes have suffered from mental illness, and many have been extremely vocal about their struggle. The WNBA's Chamique Holdsclaw; the NBA's Lamar Odom, Delonte West, Metta World Peace; and the NFL's Quincy Carter, Eddie George, and Keith O'Neil have all shared their mental illness stories with the public. Some miss the adrenaline rush of game day, others miss the comradery of their teammates, and several others miss the financial security of a steady paycheck. As this conversation continues, listen to the athletes who tell their stories and how seeking help saved their lives.

You will experience highs and lows in your career, and your survival will depend on your preparation for the lows.

Although mental illness can be treated with psychotherapy and/or medication, many athletes engage in self-destructive behavior to cope with their illness. They turn to drugs, alcohol, insubordination, financial overspending, and risky behavior with the opposite sex. By the time they realize that they need help, it's typically too late. Whenever I hear about athletes engaging in this type of reckless behavior, I immediately wonder what the underlying issue could be. Those outward behaviors are usually symptoms of the problem.

I encourage all athletes to talk to a mental health professional to help them uncover and address any mental health issues. Do not risk your lifelong health and well-being for money.

This is your legacy; this is your life; this is your chance to lead others who are afraid to get the help they need.

 Talk to a mental health professional outside your school or team if you suspect you are having trouble dealing with certain feelings. Remember, mental health professionals are bound by confidentiality codes. Eliminate fear from your decision and put your overall health first. The sooner you address a mental illness issue, the healthier you will be. Utilize the treatment course recommended for you to avoid any lapses or setbacks.

Chapter 6

Preserving Physical Health for Longevity

 How should I take care of my body for long-term health?

"Wisdom is always an overmatch for strength."

–Former NBA player and legendary coach, Phil Jackson

-6-

Many of you have spent your entire lives playing sports. Most programs will accept youth as young as four years old, and while that early start gives you more time to sharpen your skills, it also puts more wear on your body. It is very important that you understand how to take care of your body for maximum performance and career longevity. Your diet, your training methods, and your injury maintenance will dictate your quality of life long after you retire from your sport.

There is no substitute for hard work and discipline. None! While it may be tempting to take a legal or illegal substance to try to gain an edge, the temporary surge is never worth the long-term damage. Many substances are highly addictive, and every performance-enhancing drug or supplement has potential side effects. Trying to solve one issue is likely to create another. Although this seems like common sense, many professional athletes use supplements, drugs, and alcohol to improve their performance, deal with pain, or cope with stress. It is worth remembering that you are responsible for everything that goes into your body. You are responsible for the benefits and the consequences!

To combat substance abuse and the use of performance-enhancing drugs (PEDs), the NFL has instituted league policies to regulate the players' drug use. The league policies cover banned substances, marijuana test thresholds, conviction suspensions, confidentiality breaches, arbitration guidelines, and more. The drug tests can be conducted randomly and on any day except game day.

NFL policies for substance abuse and performance-enhancing drugs differ mainly in how they are enforced. Penalties for violating the PEDs policy can result in a player entering an enhanced testing and treatment program, fines, and in repeat offender scenarios, suspensions.

Consequences for violating the NFL's substance abuse policy are much more stringent, and initial offenses carry multi-game suspensions. While several companies advertise their drug or its ingredients as being on the respective leagues' "approved substances lists," it's always a good practice to take only those prescribed by the team physician or trainer.

While many NFL players attempt to "beat the test," the consequences of a failed result can be devastating. In the 2015 NFL Combine, former Nebraska star Randy Gregory—expected by some to be a Top-10 pick in the 2015 NFL draft—tested positive for marijuana. Although he was ultimately drafted as the sixtieth overall pick in the second round, it can be argued that his test results cost him millions of dollars. Josh Gordon, a Cleveland Browns receiver, missed the entire 2015 NFL season after testing positive for alcohol. However, before being reinstated for the 2016 NFL season, Gordon failed another drug test, testing positive for marijuana through a diluted sample he provided. There is no drug worth missing valuable years of your career, especially when it does more harm than good to your body.

The NBA's drug policy is harsher for violating both PEDs and substance abuse guidelines. OJ Mayo is one NBA player who suffered severe consequences for violating the league's drug policy. Mayo had an extensive history of violations that eventually earned him a two-season ban! In 2011, he was suspended ten games for testing positive for PEDs, which he attributed to an energy drink. His 2016 violation was suspected to be caused by cocaine use. The use of these drugs will affect Mayo's body long after his career ends. Do not ever underestimate the power of these drugs to become addictive and destroy your life. Even the strongest, most well-paid athletes have struggled to overcome various addictions and have had to live with deteriorating health.

Oftentimes, drugs are used to cope with various injuries. Due to the physical nature of the NFL and NBA, players will likely experience injuries that may plague them their entire lives. Because of conditions such as knee surgeries, back injuries, and head injuries, athletes can take legal and approved pain medications to help them perform at a high level during the rigorous season. The problem is that your body will build up a resistance to these medications due to overuse, creating a dependency where you cannot perform without them. One of the main culprits is cortisone shots that are administered to the site of an injury to deliver a high dosage of medicine for nearly instantaneous pain and anti-inflammatory relief. Although there are medical guidelines for its use due to the side effects, this short-term fix is highly overused in professional sports.

If a professional athlete is injured, medical personnel faces significant pressure to get the athlete back on the field or court quickly. Sometimes this puts medical trainers in a difficult situation, because while their ethical duty is to protect you, the pressure from management forces them to keep you on the field or court. My college career was riddled with injuries, in part because I didn't take the time to adequately heal. If you have an injury, make sure you get the rest and treatment you need to fully recover. You cannot be afraid to get a second opinion because you know your body better than anyone else. Forcing yourself to play through what could develop into a potentially serious injury for a team's short-term needs can contribute to a lifetime of pain and resentment.

The most controversial injury in the NFL is CTE, a degenerative disease found in those that have had repeated blows to the head, which we mentioned earlier. Until recently, the NFL had failed to acknowledge there is a link between football and CTE, which may explain the league's lack of initiative in taking responsibility for protecting and treating its active and retired players. Studies on the brains of several athletes have shown that most of the high school, collegiate, professional, retired, and even deceased football athletes that were sampled have suffered from CTE. Symptoms of the disease can begin years after the injury and include headaches, dizziness, disorientation, memory loss, erratic behavior, and poor judgment. Although you may be able to play soon after suffering a head injury, think about the long-term effects of repeated blows. Currently, there is no cure for CTE, and the disease gets progressively worse. There is treatment for the symptoms, but battling this disease will entail a lifetime of pain and frustration. Take it seriously; your life depends on it!

 You must do the work required to take care of your body for peak performance, career longevity, and quality of life. This includes following a healthy diet, sustainable training programs, and appropriate injury rehabilitation programs. Resist the urge to take shortcuts with performance-enhancing drugs and illegal substances as these substances will not only violate league drug policies, they also have the potential to become addictive and harmful to your long-term health. If you are injured, get your treatment plan in writing from a certified medical professional, and take the time you need to heal. Study the effects of CTE, and take any head injury very seriously.

Chapter 7

Maintaining Relationships with the Opposite Sex

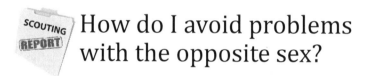 How do I avoid problems with the opposite sex?

"Do your best when no one is looking. If you do that, then you can be successful in anything that you put your mind to."
–Former NBA guard, Kevin Johnson

-7-

Relationships with family, mental health issues, and the stress of physical injuries can influence how an athlete deals with those of the opposite sex. Many times, if you grew up without one parent's guidance in your life, you will miss the lessons of how to value, interact with, and treat your companions. As your athletic potential grows, you may be treated as the breadwinner or "man" of the house, oftentimes being treated like your single mother's companion versus her child. You may have a relationship with both parents, but the relationships are highly dysfunctional. Some athletes use their personal relationships as an outlet for their pain, frustration, and stress. These broken personal relationships have made cheating, child support, and domestic violence topics of debate in the sports world.

The fast, luxurious lifestyle of an athlete is attractive to spectators and especially to groupies, female fans who are more interested in a relationship with an athlete because of his status. These women are usually very attractive, and they spend time in various places that professional athletes congregate, such as parties and post-game events. They typically seduce athletes for access into their world for financial gain or status. It is hard for an athlete to resist being inundated with available sex. Many athletes are tempted by these women, and their lack of control has cost them greatly.

Oftentimes, these women will perceive a one-time encounter as an ongoing relationship. She may follow you and mysteriously show up in places you frequent to persuade you to continue a relationship with her. It may happen so often that you feel the need to protect yourself legally and/ or physically.

Think about the worst-case scenario before you connect with someone you barely know, especially when alcohol, drugs, or sex is involved in the introduction.

Many athletes have underestimated the power of these situations to ruin their lives and have had to deal with public scrutiny, family shame, and career distraction years after the occurrence.

A great number of athletes are in relationships and still cheat on their partners. Some veteran athletes believe that it is an unspoken part of the culture of professional sports, leading young rookies to blindly engage in risky behavior with women. There is no infidelity worth losing a loyal partner or your family's support, so take the proper precautions to avoid uncomfortable situations. It is very difficult to fight your natural physical responses to sexual temptations, so do everything in your power to remove yourself from tempting situations before they escalate. These personal problems will distract the most focused professional athlete, so never think of yourself as immune. With the technological advances of social media, these secret encounters can and have become public in the most embarrassing way possible.

One tactic that I have seen fail miserably for professional athletes is to have their sexual encounters covered under a legal contract. BEFORE engaging in the sexual encounter, the woman must sign a contract prohibiting her from discussing the encounter with anyone, contacting the athlete afterwards, or ever suing him for any type of financial relief or otherwise. If she breaches the contract, she can be pursued legally. In some of the cases, allegations of rape, pregnancy, or STD transmittal have made those contracts null and void and, ultimately, a public nightmare. Make the right choice, and avoid using a legal contract to cover infidelity and unprotected sex. Better yet, avoid infidelity and unprotected sex altogether.

Sometimes a child is conceived from these dalliances. If you and the child's mother were not married and were not in a relationship when the child was conceived, you may have a legal child-support battle on your hands. What's more, the woman may have baited you for this result all along because there are women out there whose life purpose is to have a child with a professional athlete and live off the support they receive. This legal action could also be retaliation for the failed relationship. However, your status and high-income make it very likely that you will be pursued for paternity and child support. Legally, both biological parents of a child have a duty to support the child until the age of majority or until parental rights have been legally terminated.

Antonio Cromartie, who was selected in the 2006 NFL draft, fathered twelve children with nine women. Although he was regarded as one of the best cornerbacks in the NFL, he had serious issues off the field and now pays over $336,000 each year in child support!

In 2010, he even asked the New York Jets for a $500,000 advance to help him pay his child-support bills! The NBA's Shawn Kemp is also known for more than his basketball skills. Nicknamed "Reign Man" for his physical play and dunking ability, Kemp allegedly fathered at least seven children with six women.

Your lifestyle and financial soundness will influence the amount of support that is set. I always remind athletes of this because those lavish lifestyles work against them when a judge evaluates their ability to pay a set support amount. Because a professional athlete's lifestyle usually changes dramatically once he retires, players can accumulate massive legal fees in their attempts to lower their child-support obligations. This process could drag on for years and threaten your post-career financial security. When you had millions coming in, you could afford six-figure support payments. However, once those checks stop coming, it doesn't take long to exhaust any savings. With some athletes paying north of $40,000 per month in child support, it is no wonder this is one of the main causes of the high post-career financial hardship statistics. Some athletes have filed bankruptcy, and others have even been arrested for failure to pay child support. This is another way to taint a strong legacy and introduce mental health issues, such as depression.

I urge all athletes to fight for visitation and noncustodial parental rights for their children. Regardless of the financial implications of the child's conception, that child still needs the influence of both parents in its life. I have witnessed many athletes consume themselves with the fight over money at the expense of the well-being of their child. Your visitation and parental rights are separate from child support, so make sure your attorney includes those issues in any settlement. Many times, a vindictive mother will use the child as a weapon because the father is not aware of his options to enforce his legal rights. If all else fails, pursue a healthy relationship with your child to prevent another broken child or athlete from repeating the same mistakes in their lifetime.

When the money is gone, your relationship
with your child will be the most
rewarding gift you will ever receive.

Domestic violence, as it pertains to athletes and their relationships with the opposite sex, is another topic receiving increased media attention. It is never acceptable for any man to physically assault a woman or child. Ever! While the NFL and NBA try to maintain their distance from the personal affairs of their players, both leagues have had to institute policies and issue suspensions when dealing with domestic abuse.

Recently, the NFL's Adrian Peterson was reprimanded for allegedly physically abusing his son. Peterson admitted to disciplining his son, although he didn't intend to leave visible marks on the child. Ray Rice was punished for striking his wife when the incident was caught on an elevator camera. Chad Ochocinco's physical assault on his wife, which required the police to be called, ultimately ended his playing career. It is likely that stress—and possibly privilege—contributed to the escalation of these situations.

Many expect NFL players to engage in violent behavior due to the growing number of head injuries in football. However, NBA players are subject to the same pressures that cause the breakdowns that lead to domestic abuse. The Boston Celtics' Jared Sullinger was arrested following a domestic dispute with his girlfriend in 2013. In the same year, ex-NBA player Craig Ehlo was arrested for felony domestic abuse, while current NBA player Darren Collison pled guilty to domestic violence for striking his wife in 2016.

The media attention that these incidences receive contributes to the stress on athletes, making it more likely that they will repeat this unacceptable behavior. Again, usually these outbursts signal an underlying struggle that needs immediate attention and treatment to prevent further physical assaults.

Although many athletes experience stress, financial loss, and legal trouble when dealing with the opposite sex, this does not describe all the professional athlete relationships in the NBA and NFL. Many athletes have sustained long, fulfilling relationships and respectful marriages. The NBA's Doug Christie and Alonzo Mourning have been married for twenty-one and twenty years, respectively. The NFL's Emmitt Smith has been married for seventeen years. Some of these women have been around since before the fame, and others have formed loyal relationships since the athlete's rise to stardom. A good number of athletes use measures to keep their private life private to avoid the stress on their relationship that comes with being in the public eye. It can surely be done, and your career, financial security, and peace of mind will thrive when you handle your personal life accordingly.

Due to the high financial stakes involved in being in a relationship as a professional athlete, you should consider a prenuptial agreement. Unless your personal or religious beliefs prohibit this type of contractual protection, I suggest you discuss this with an attorney. No one enters a marriage planning for it to end, but when it does, you want to ensure you have secured your financial security, in addition to that of your wife and children. If you never divorce, the agreement is not an issue. While you may not actually enter into a prenuptial agreement, gathering information from legal counsel can help you make an informed decision.

 Revisit the list you created about your legacy. If you did not include child-support issues, cheating scandals, promiscuity, or domestic-violence arrests, take every step you can to prevent those vices from ruining your life and your career. Visualize your reaction if your private text messages, conversations, and activities were made public. Be honest in your communication with those of the opposite sex, and take great care to remove yourself from potentially compromising situations. Remove family and friends from your circle that put you in positions to compromise your character.

Chapter 8

Understanding Cash Flow, Taxes, & Contract Guarantees

 How important is cash flow to my financial security?

"I like to call it tunnel vision. It's not good to have tunnel vision on the field, because you need to know what's going on around you, but when you're in life, especially in this field, you need to have tunnel vision, because you see so many guys around you buying cars, buying jewelry, doing this, spending money, talking about the money that they spend."

–NFL safety, Glover Quin

-8-

When you evaluate the many reasons that athletes experience financial hardship, you might conclude that most have a poor understanding of basic financial concepts. These athletes make long-term decisions based on short-term income. Most of them use their total contract and endorsement figures to determine if they can afford the items that they purchase. However, there are several important considerations that should factor into any short-term decision-making and long-term financial planning. Some of these considerations are net worth, cash flow, budgeting, taxes, and contract guarantees.

Generally, you should make financial decisions and investments that improve your net worth, which is your overall financial value at a point in time. It is calculated by adding all your assets (your cash on hand and the value of all the things you own) and then subtracting your liabilities (the total value of everything that you owe). A positive net worth indicates that you own more than you owe to others. A negative net worth indicates that you owe to others more than you own. Decisions that improve your net worth are those that increase your cash on hand and what you own and those that decrease what you owe to others.

Although the net-worth calculation gives a snapshot overview of financial value, the most overlooked assessment of an athlete's financial health is a cash-flow analysis. Cash flow is the net amount of cash and cash-equivalent instruments moving in and out of your financial picture. This analysis shows you how much cash you have available after covering all your expenses. A positive cash flow indicates that your assets are increasing, enabling you to pay your expenses, save, AND invest. A negative cash flow suggests that you are living beyond your means and that you will eventually have to borrow money to cover your expenses. Future income is not included in the cash-flow calculation, even though many athletes erroneously make financial decisions based on what they expect to earn in the future, rather than their present cash flow. They are spending money they don't yet have! Those poor calculations will eventually lead to financial problems because you are spending more than you have available.

Once you determine that you have a positive cash flow, you must determine how you will allocate the excess cash. The cash-flow number is closely related to and very important in determining an athlete's budget, savings plan, and investment capability over a period of time. A budget is a plan for your future income and expenses that you use as a guideline for your spending and savings. Essentially, you set aside a certain amount of money for various expenses to help you control your spending. It is the only practical way to understand where your money goes and to ensure it is being spent the way you intend. Effective budgeting requires you to review your actual income and expenses versus what you forecasted so that you can adjust if you are spending more than you budgeted. Many athletes fail to make a budget, and those that do oftentimes neglect to follow up to see if they operated within their proposed guidelines. As simple as the budgeting concept is, it is only as effective as you make it!

Many athletes also fail to account for federal and state taxes in their spending decisions. Because of a professional athlete's high income, they usually fall into the highest federal tax bracket. A good rule of thumb is to subtract half your salary and endorsement earnings to account for tax withholding. Yes, I said HALF! In addition to paying various federal taxes, you will also have to pay a "jock tax" in each state where you compete and earn income. This is the reason many athletes buy a home in one of the nine states without state income tax because state taxes are determined based on your state of residence. The nine states without state income tax are Alaska, Florida, Nevada, South Dakota, Texas, Washington, Wyoming, Tennessee, and New Hampshire. So if you set your primary residence in one of these states, you can avoid paying state taxes in each state where your team competes.

Understanding taxes and cash flow can help professional athletes avoid many financial problems. Many times, athletes make mental commitments to purchase expensive items and support family members and friends when they sign a contract for a large salary because, initially, they do not consider how much of their salary will go to taxes. They also fail to realize how several smaller, recurring expenses can collectively create a monthly outlay that will be hard to maintain.

While you should learn about basic financial concepts as soon as possible, I think it is important to take a step back to explore the misconceptions that exist BEFORE you sign your first deal. Usually, athletes spend more time planning what they want to purchase with their first professional paycheck than understanding how their draft status will impact their base salary and contract guarantees. I urge you to make sure that your agent is also an attorney, has one on his staff, or is at least well versed in the CBA and other contractual matters. Both the NFL and the NBA have CBAs, or collective bargaining agreements, to set guidelines for player contracts and rookie salary caps. These agreements cover team rights, player rights, and salary scales. In addition to the protections set in the CBA, most agents will attempt to include protections against injury or lack of skill.

The NBA draft is an annual event usually held in June. Sixty athletes are selected over two rounds, with contract guarantees for first-round selections. If you are picked as one of the first ten selections in the draft—the lottery picks— your contract is guaranteed, and your enhanced base salary is pre-set based on your draft number. These athletes usually receive lucrative marketing endorsements as well.

If you are chosen as picks eleven through thirty, your salary is still guaranteed and set based on your draft number.

Second-round draft picks have lower salary minimums, and their contracts are NOT guaranteed. So it is possible to be drafted in the second round but not make a final roster.

If you are not drafted, you can still be picked up by an NBA team to showcase your talents during the NBA Summer Leagues or team workouts. However, you may still be cut in training camp or sent to an NBA Developmental League affiliate team for the season. While you may receive call-ups to an active roster throughout the season, your pay in the NBA Developmental League is NOTHING like that of those signed to the active roster of an NBA team. I know players in the NBA Development League that played for $40,000 per season! If you do make an NBA roster, did you know that you won't receive your first paycheck until November? Many athletes get into debt, spending money before they receive their first salary payment.

It is of the upmost importance for you to understand that even after you sign your contract, it still may not be fully guaranteed. There are clauses in NBA and NFL contracts that dictate several reasons they can use to potentially void portions of your professional contract. For the most part, the NBA fully guarantees its contracts upon signing, although they can still waive a player or have their contract bought out. The NBA's Gilbert Arenas signed a deal with the Washington Wizards worth over $100 million. He collected the entire amount, despite several serious knee injuries, a nearly full-season suspension, and a gun-related felony charge.

Now, the NFL has very different stipulations for its draft, contracts, and salary guarantees. The NFL draft is also an annual event, usually held over three days in late April or early May. The 253 athletes are selected over seven rounds, with the first round being held on Day One, the second and third rounds being held on Day Two, and the fourth through seventh rounds held on Day Three. In general, NFL base salaries are not fully guaranteed. There are total contract figures, then there are guaranteed figures. Know the difference! Essentially, the "guarantees" are dependent on if you are on the team at the time it is due to be paid. NFL players bear more salary risk than those in any other professional sport. Even the top picks in the NFL draft may have some base salary guarantees for only the first couple years, but usually the league doesn't make long-term commitments to its players. Signing bonuses aren't necessarily guaranteed, but because you are usually paid immediately, the league cannot retract its payment. Roster bonuses are not guaranteed either, but if you are still on the roster past a certain date, it's yours.

Even if you are not selected in the NFL draft, you still have opportunities to make a final roster. You are categorized as an undrafted free agent, and you will have workout, combine, and training-camp opportunities to impress team executives to earn a chance to make their roster or practice squad. You should know there is a substantial difference in salary for an NFL active player at league minimum ($450,000 in 2016) and a practice squad player ($117,300 in 2016). Again, you will not receive your first check until the regular season begins in late August, and roster cuts can be made up until that time. The teams must cut to a fifty-three-man roster, and even if you make the final team, you could still be sent to the practice squad throughout the season. Because NFL players are paid weekly over the seventeen-game season, their pay can depend on which team they are on that week. For example, a player on the active roster may receive 1/17 of their salary one week, then receive 1/17 of the practice squad salary the next week. There is not much job security, so you should consider this in any purchase decisions and commitments.

The NFL has a lot more flexibility to relieve itself of its contractual obligations to its players for several reasons, such as poor performance, poor attitudes, or if they feel a player simply isn't worth a deal that was put in place years ago, because the NFL and its players can restructure contracts. Again, most NFL contracts have only partial guarantees anyway, so if they decide they no longer need your services after paying the guaranteed amount of your contract, they can forego paying you the unguaranteed balance left on your contract. For example, if a player signs a $20,000,000 deal, with $10,000,000 guaranteed, paid as a $5,000,000 annual salary over 4-years, and is released after year two, the team would owe NOTHING beyond the $10,000,000 paid. That's right: NOTHING!

This is astonishing, given the physical landscape of the sport and the long-term effects it has on its players' minds and bodies. Not understanding the guarantees in your contract can leave you ill prepared to deal with a sudden injury or change of heart. Most NFL players talk about the pressure they feel not only every season but every game because of their lack of job security. With the help of a qualified attorney who is versed in your sports CBA, get to know and understand the protection clauses in your contract.

 Learn about basic financial concepts, such as net worth, cash flow, and budgeting, to make strong short-term and long-term financial decisions. Understand how taxes and contract guarantees impact your take-home pay and contract longevity. Perform financial assessments regularly (at least monthly), and make the necessary adjustments to keep yourself on track for your goals.

Do not make a long-term decision
based on short-term income!

Chapter 9

Using Wisdom in Your Savings, Investments, & Asset Protection Strategies

 How do I make better financial decisions to avoid hardship?

"People complain that professional athletes make a lot of money, but what they don't understand is that we need a lot of money because we spend a lot of money."

–Retired NBA Hall of Famer, Patrick Ewing

-9-

After spending a decade in the financial-planning industry, I can tell you that most individuals make financial decisions based on emotion rather than logic. This is especially true of professional athletes who come into large sums of money very quickly.

I always tell my clients, "Your bank account doesn't make you rich—your behavior does."

What good is the most financially rewarding gift if you don't know how to keep it?

After being around sports my entire life, I am still amazed that individuals who utilize such a high level of discipline in their athletic endeavors can be so undisciplined in their financial decisions. You don't get up at 4:00 a.m. to train or go on a strict diet because you want to; you do it because you believe it will help you get an edge on the court or field. As I wrote earlier, these preconceptions about money and its value are usually set in your childhood. It is always easier to create a new habit than it is to break an old one. The problem is, most athletes don't take the time to break their old money habits to relearn new strategies. Truthfully, most financial professionals don't take the time to establish a strong educational foundation with their clients, either.

Because of your high income, you are a target for scheming advisors. If you suffer some small loss, you may not immediately see it due to your busy schedule, so you are unaware of any poor advice or fraudulent acts. You may forget to keep a close eye on your finances, and before you know it, everyone around you is blaming you for your poor decision-making. Well, I blame YOU for your poor choice of professionals, for choosing people who worked to gain your trust but not educate you. I blame you for not having checks and balances on your team. I blame you for not asking questions to educate yourself!

Because money represents power, athletes oftentimes participate in risky investments.

Again, this is the emotional context that frames what you can do with money, rather than what money can do for you. It is no secret that your professional career will most likely span less than a decade, meaning you must live off your savings for a period of time that is at least five times the length of your career. So why would you risk your financial security for a gamble to accumulate more money than you could ever dream of spending? I will say it again—for power. And in your quest for more, you will most likely lose yourself and a lot of your investment in the process. Remember when I asked you to determine what would make you lower your standards? You will be tempted even after you've made it to the big league.

To remove the emotional pressure in money matters and implement discipline into any financial regimen, I have my clients utilize direct deposit and automatic transfer tools. Many top athletes use these basic strategies to help them control their spending and force them to save. The idea is that you are less likely to spend what you never see. Your salary payments are deposited directly into one of your accounts, but budgeted amounts are transferred to your other accounts for various purposes. At a minimum, you should have an account for bill payment and an account for your personal spending. I know players with several accounts for purposes such as summer vacations, business dealings, and even family emergencies. Many athletes try to make all transactions from one account and easily overspend each month. When it's gone, it's gone!

It is important to know that you can save money without investing, but you shouldn't invest without first saving. Anytime there is the smallest chance that you could lose some of your investment without doing anything, you should think about what you would do in that worst-case scenario. Oftentimes, when someone recommends an investment to you, they discuss only the positive aspects. Examples of savings instruments are savings accounts, money-market accounts, certificates of deposit (CDs), insurance policies, and savings bonds. These types of investments are relatively safe and allow you to earn some interest. Most importantly, you are protected against loss up to certain limits. Examples of investments are stocks, bonds, mutual funds, real estate, commodities, options, and business investments. While you could make a substantial amount of money with these types of investments, there is also great potential for losing your original investment. In even the soundest investment decisions, there are so many variables out of your control that can affect your return. There is risk in everything, so never overlook the risk for the reward!

If you understand how an investment works, the risks associated with it, your alternatives to it, and you readily accept it, then you have no one to blame for any misfortune but yourself. But remember, when you have others depending on your stability and you put yourself in such an unstable position, you could live with the guilt of a bad decision forever. When you are comparing investments, my advice is to write down the pros and cons of each and the potential loss and gain, using real numbers. Then, make your decision based on the least probability of loss rather than the greatest possibility of gain. Once you are more educated about financial instruments and have a consistent income, you can take more risk in your investments. Until then, be as conservative as possible. Athletes are investing large sums of money in the technology field because they've "heard about all the money you could make there." Unfortunately, that's not a good basis for a financial decision, and there are equal—if not more—investors who have lost money in that sector. Educate yourself!

Asset protection should be the most important financial goal to any professional athlete. You will have plenty of opportunities to take risks during your career, so do not neglect to protect your most valuable assets. At one point, the NFL's Troy Polamalu insured his hair! He had several marketing endorsements because of it, so he decided to protect one of his streams of income. In all fairness, this sport is your livelihood, your life, and your legacy. Protect it or lose it!

Although asset protection seems to be a common-sense topic, many athletes fail to protect themselves and their lives due to miseducation and procrastination. Several athletes have died without life insurance or a will to determine how their assets will be divided among their family, leading to financial distress and chaos tainting their memory and legacy upon their death. NFL player Steve McNair was killed by his alleged girlfriend in 2009, leaving a wife, children, and no will. In addition to living with the pain of losing a loved one and the shock of finding out about his extramarital affair, his widow was forced to have some of his assets unfrozen by the courts to care for the children.

While the NBA and NFL offer life insurance, disability coverage, and pension benefits, it is always a good idea for you to explore obtaining more coverage. Your life insurance policy will leave money to your beneficiary should something happen to you, and oftentimes the league coverage is not enough to cover your debt, burial expenses, and lifestyle to provide income to your family. With coverage for physical disabilities becoming a more widely addressed topic in both leagues, it will also benefit you to explore additional disability coverage. Again, whether you purchase it is up to you, but do your homework to make an informed decision. Most insurance premiums are less expensive the younger you are when you secure them, so it is always a good idea to learn the benefits and assess the costs early in your career to lock in low rates. Moreover, ensure that you have savings and investments in place to supplement your pension benefits so that you can sustain your lifestyle in retirement. For athletes, retirement age can be as early as thirty!

While there are several common financial strategies used with athletes, many turn to real estate as their primary investment. The reasoning is that real estate appreciates over time and has the potential to create consistent cash flow. However, many athletes have lost millions of dollars in real estate deals because of its illiquidity, market risks, and the interest paid on financing. It is very difficult to cash out of a real estate deal quickly. Although your specific investments may differ, you should have an investment mix that at least outpaces inflation, which is a sustained increase in the price level of goods and services over time. For example, you can purchase much less with twenty dollars today than you could ten years ago. You have the same amount of money, but because the prices of things have gone up over time, you are forced to purchase fewer goods. So, putting money under a mattress can hurt you in the long run if you do not have a good mix of savings and investments that grow.

Retired NBA player Antoine Walker is most famous for squandering over $100 million in earnings. In 2010, Walker filed for Chapter 7 bankruptcy protection in the Southern District of Florida. He had to sell his championship ring to cover debts on various real-estate properties, gambling debts, and other legal debts. Allegedly, Walker spent millions of dollars over his career financing his relatives and supporting many of his friends. In 2013, Walker announced that he was debt-free and is now a basketball analyst on a sports broadcast.

Poor financial decisions and meager management have also affected various NFL players over the years. Vince Young played in the NFL for six seasons and earned over $34 million in salary and over $30 million in endorsement deals over his career, yet in 2014, Young filed bankruptcy in a Houston federal bankruptcy court. He began experiencing financial problems after defaulting on a high-interest payday loan with a lender for professional athletes. While he eventually settled with his creditors, his financial troubles took a toll on his mental health, his family, and his legacy.

However, not all professional athletes make poor financial decisions. Magic Johnson is one athlete that has achieved great success on and off the court. He has started a record label, worked as a motivational speaker, commentated for the NBA, created a prepaid MasterCard for low-income people, invested in various real estate development projects, and became a minority owner in several sports teams, such as the Los Angeles Lakers, the Los Angeles Dodgers, and the Los Angeles Sparks. He began exploring why so many athletes fail in business while he was still playing for the NBA's Los Angeles Lakers. After seeking the advice of a top business professional, Johnson began reading about business, exploring his network, and meeting with executives as much as possible—even during road games. Johnson's decision to arm himself with information BEFORE making investments has paid off for him and his legacy.

 Hire a competent, trustworthy advisor and review with them often. Write out your financial goals and plans to achieve them. Break down your activities, budget by the week, and measure your progress. Make sure to secure life and disability coverage as soon as possible, and contribute regularly to a retirement savings plan. Make real-estate and other risky investments with only a small percentage of your income and only after you've educated yourself and evaluated the pros and cons.

Chapter 10

Preserving Good Credit

 How can I maintain good credit? Why should I?

*"Excellence is not a
singular act but a habit.
You are what you do repeatedly."*

–NBA legend, Shaquille O'Neal

-10-

The most important financial advice I can offer is to learn all you can about any financial topic that interests, involves, and affects you. One often-overlooked financial topic is credit. For individuals who make millions of dollars a year, credit health may seem like an unnecessary tool to understand. You have enough money to buy what you want, so why do you need to concern yourself with credit?

Credit is your track record of keeping your end of the bargain in financial commitments. When credit is extended to you, you agree to pay back the loan under terms that set the recurring payment amount, the interest or finance charges, and the time schedule required to satisfy the debt. Your credit score is important because it determines what loans you qualify for and what interest rate you will pay.

Three companies monitor your credit by requiring those that have extended credit to you to report if you are paying back your debt as agreed: Experian, Equifax, and Transunion. They assign a three-digit credit score that is also used to set your insurance rates, to determine if you can rent an apartment, and even to assess your character. If you have a poor credit history, this means that you have broken your promises in some manner to repay borrowed funds, such as mortgage loans, auto loans, or credit cards. This indicates that a lender will risk not receiving their loan back if they decide to lend to you. Usually, you will pay a higher fee if credit is extended to you to compensate them for the risk they assume by entering into an agreement with you.

Lenders do consider an athlete's high income in assessing their ability to repay any debts. However, income alone cannot replace a poor credit rating. This mismatch of high income and poor credit taints a lender's confidence in your willingness to pay. After all, if you have the funds available, why haven't you repaid your debts per your agreed-upon terms?

Many times, athletes are affected by poor credit for several reasons: (1) they have made poor past financial decisions and were unable to repay them as agreed; (2) they were victims of fraud; or (3) they have hired unqualified people to handle the payments to their creditors. These negative marks on their credit report can be improved, but unfortunately, it takes time.

I have seen many athletes fall into a credit trap in college by opening several credit cards, not considering how they would pay them off. College students are prey for credit-card issuers because they usually have a need for additional cash. The credit-card companies will lure in unsuspecting, naïve students and charge incredible interest rates when they use the cards. Always read the fine print!

Right out of college, athletes are also vulnerable to "runners" looking to sign them to an agent with whom they work. They may give them money or things to entice their commitment, but if the athlete chooses to work with another agent, the runner can sue the athlete to repay all the cash and gifts they received. The legal judgment can even appear on their credit report. Never take anything from anyone because everything comes with a price. Those pre-draft cars, gifts, and cash loans from your agent usually have to be repaid – most often, with interest.

Because professional athletes usually keep a lot of people around them, they are high-risk targets for theft and fraud. From parties to group dinners, women and men alike have stolen money, credit cards, and even identification documents from athletes to steal from them or impersonate them. When alcohol and drugs are involved, it is hard for you to discern who could've been involved. In many cases, close relatives and friends have stolen from the athletes that provide for them and, unbeknownst to the athlete, opened accounts in their names. The "loyalty complex" makes it hard for an athlete to legally pursue a loved one, and many athletes elect to take the hit to their credit rather than prosecute.

Oftentimes, athletes hire individuals (though not always professionals) to pay their bills and make payments to creditors. When you hire unqualified, unorganized people, you run the risk of late payments, missed payments, and even legal judgments that you don't know about ruining your credit worthiness. I have worked with athletes who had items on their credit report that they didn't find out were there until they went to apply for a loan. Getting denied was a shocking surprise!

Sometimes athletes pay cash for everything to avoid paying additional interest on debt. However, utilizing debt to acquire certain things can work to your advantage by leveraging your assets. You can use borrowed funds to make purchases and keep your cash. Leverage is when an asset is purchased using borrowed funds, with the assumption that the income (or appreciation in value) from the asset will be more than the cost of the loan. Keep in mind that if you borrow too much, the payments on your loans can still cripple your cash flow. Understand how debt can help you accomplish your financial goals before committing to a long-term repayment schedule for a loan.

Remember, it is easier to protect your credit than it is to rebuild it, and you can do several things to protect your credit. One important activity is to check your credit annually. Everyone can receive one free credit report from the three credit bureaus each year to review the accuracy of information on their credit report. The website to receive the reports is www.annualcreditreport.com.

It is also a good idea to set up credit monitoring to alert you to any changes to your credit report as they occur. When you are alerted of a new account that you didn't open, you have the option to dispute it with the credit company. They have thirty days to respond to your dispute and will request proof of the new account information to evaluate the claim.

Make sure you pay all your bills on time or at least within thirty days past its due date to avoid having the negative item reported to the credit companies. Additionally, avoid borrowing too much or applying for too many credit cards in a short period of time because that suggests to lenders that you are cash-strapped and may not be able to repay them.

Lastly, try to keep your account balances at 30 percent of the limit, as high, maxed-out credit lines indicate that you are having trouble paying your debts. Surprisingly, paying accounts to zero can hurt you because it doesn't show the lender that you can maintain debt month to month.

Your credit is important because it not only assesses your likelihood of repaying your debts, but it also reflects your character. In general, athletes with poor credit are seen as unreliable and financially irresponsible. Consequently, athletes with good credit are seen as dependable and responsible. Employers, landlords, and insurers are increasingly relying on credit scores to make important assumptions about you. Protect yours at all costs!

Understand how your credit is used to evaluate your character and your financial health, and use it wisely. Take the necessary precautions to safeguard your personal information and financial instruments against theft and fraud, and check your credit regularly to stay abreast of changes to your report. Check your report annually, and sign up for a monthly credit-monitoring service. Be careful about opening new credit cards if you can't afford to pay off what you charge each month. One mistake can take years to correct, so be proactive about protecting your credit rating as early as your college years!

Chapter 11

Developing a Post-Career Skill Early

 How do I begin preparing for what I will do when I retire?

*"Today I will do what others won't,
so tomorrow I can accomplish
what others can't."*

–NFL Hall of Famer, Jerry Rice

-11-

You will learn several skills and life lessons from your sports journey that can be applied to any field. For instance, you acquire sound time-management skills by balancing your classwork and your athletic obligations. Operating in a team atmosphere enables you to develop social skills and learn how to work with individuals with different personalities and backgrounds. Furthermore, a certain level of confidence is required to perform and make mistakes in front of a crowd of people. These skills make you one of the most valuable hires to companies around the world. In general, your athletic background indicates that you are goal-oriented, relentless in your pursuit of a goal, and learn things quickly.

While playing sports can enhance your skill set, it can also enrich your life experience. Basketball, football, and other sports can be used to finance your college education, to introduce you to famous people, and to allow you to travel to different parts of the world. If you excel among your peers, you could even make a lot of money by simply playing a game that you love. But, most importantly, you can use your platform as a professional athlete to touch lives while pursuing one of your other passions. This passion can help you create a stream of income that can provide for you and your family into retirement.

Because you can declare for the NBA draft once you reach the age of nineteen and are at least one year removed from high school (or playing one collegiate season), and you can be eligible for the NFL draft once you are three years removed from high school (or playing three collegiate seasons), you will most likely need additional credit hours to complete your degree if you enter the draft early. I urge you to create a plan to finish your degree requirements during the off-season and set a completion date to work toward. Although some athletes experience some success without completing their degree, it eventually becomes a hindrance for others. As natural-born competitors, most athletes feel compelled to finish what they start, and their education is no different. When you enter the real world, you are evaluated among your peers from different backgrounds. Your lack of educational accomplishment can cause you to miss an opportunity or lose to another candidate.

Many athletes return to complete their degrees once they retire from their sport. The NFL boasts that approximately half their players have college degrees. This statistic exceeds all other professional sports, most likely because of their requirement that players be removed from high school for three years. Many NFL athletes enter the league with their college degrees while NBA and other athletes tackle their degree requirements later—usually when they are searching for work.

It took the NBA's Shaquille O'Neal eight years to return to complete his degree from Louisiana State University (LSU), but when he did return, he went on to complete his master's degree. O'Neal said in a short speech to his fellow graduates, "For people who think money and fame are important, they are only a small piece of the pie. You need an education to feel secure. I feel secure that I can get a real job now. ... I am an educated man." O'Neal didn't feel right telling kids to stay in school when he hadn't earned his own degree. Now, he can stand behind his words.

I've heard many athletes say that they don't need to finish school to be successful after their playing career, and while there are some athletes that accomplish great things without a college degree, you increase your chances tremendously by completing your degree requirements. There are several benefits to finishing college, such as increased knowledge and enhanced maturity. As you prepare for the next stage of your life, you can secure your future with a college degree.

After all, you will compete with other candidates for job openings and career opportunities. Every athlete's career has an expiration date, and achieving this important milestone will enable you to choose your next venture whether your career ends prematurely or not. It is better to have your degree and not need it than need it and not have it. Nevertheless, I can guarantee you that some part of your college experience will help you during your post-career.

You must begin thinking about your second skill NOW, as well as what is necessary to develop it into an income-producing asset to aid in your post-career transition. Many athletes procrastinate, and before they realize it, their entire career has passed them by. The problem is you will have a difficult time doing something that will earn you the same level of income you received as an elite professional athlete—only 1 percent of Americans earn those figures. So if you don't replace your income with a career in which you can earn enough to support the lifestyle you became accustomed to, you will end up in the same boat with 80 percent of NFL players and 60 percent of NBA players who experience financial problems in retirement. You can subtract from a nest egg for only so long until it's gone.

If you need help determining which career options fit your skill set, I recommend taking a career assessment test, which uses your interests and skills to determine which career paths could be a natural fit. You must start thinking about the next stage of your career NOW so that you can use the opportunities provided by your sport to prepare you for it. You will meet business professionals and potential business partners along your sports journey who can sow into your passion and help you bring your dream to reality. Remember Magic Johnson's story? He met with business leaders and executives as an active player to prepare for his post-career. Use that time wisely so that you can foster a smooth transition when the time to retire comes—because it will come, whether you are ready or not.

As you search for your second skill and passion, I suggest you find a mentor in your sport. This can be someone you know personally or someone you haven't yet met. It is important for you to have someone to bounce ideas against and to get advice from, someone who can tell you what to prepare for. It is most meaningful when that person has walked in your shoes and worn the same jersey as you have because they have firsthand experience that cannot be duplicated. Understand that this person is a part of your "power circle," and their impact on your life will be significant—although sometimes uncomfortable. Too many athletes neglect to find a mentor in their sport because they think they are prepared to navigate all that comes with being a professional athlete. However, they quickly discover how that mistake can derail or delay their post-career success.

Although professional athletes have a transferrable skill set that can be valuable in different disciplines, many settle into several common career paths. Most want to remain close to their sport, so they take up positions in coaching, training, and broadcasting. Depending on the level of coaching, most positions require a college degree. However, former athletes can train for and even enter broadcasting without receiving a college diploma. The NBA and NFL Player Associations have resources that assist athletes with post-career training and certification programs. Other common career paths include entrepreneurship, public speaking, and nonprofit fundraising.

Real estate has also emerged as a lucrative post-career option for many athletes. Although it can be extremely risky, some athletes have found success buying and renovating properties, investing in real-estate development projects, and purchasing commercial properties. This can be an appropriate venture for athletes who have accumulated substantial cash savings and have some working knowledge of the real-estate business. Some of my clients have achieved great success working with our partner groups that specialize in professional athlete real-estate acquisitions and franchise initiatives. However, because so many athletes have lost large amounts of money with speculative real-estate investments, I advise you to do your homework and proceed with the highest level of caution in any real-estate venture. While the venture can provide income, there are many variables out of your control that can disrupt the consistency and security of this income stream.

So many athletes fail to continue their success because they didn't have the support they needed at the personal level. I saw a need, so I created a solution. I made sure my team was diverse enough to focus on all the topics in this section. I believe it is imperative for you to invest in your education, skill set, and growth so that you leave your sport better than you entered it, in more areas than financial ones. My goal is to have your post-career in place BEFORE you retire. Our mentoring network with other retired athletes has been a valuable resource in accomplishing this goal. Your success will depend on your focus in all areas of your life, and your focus must extend to your future, not just your present.

 Make a list of three alternative career paths for you outside sports and the qualifications needed for each. Make a plan, complete with a timetable, to finish your degree requirements. Find a mentor in your sport who can give you useful advice and who will push you to make good decisions. Utilize real-estate opportunities wisely, and always use the resources of your league's players' association.

Chapter 12

Learning How to Reward Yourself

 How can I save money but also enjoy some of the fruit of my labor?

"I'm blessed. I'm blessed every day I wake up. So I just try to maximize every day to the fullest."

–Former NFL Super Bowl Champion, Marshawn Lynch

-12-

To repeat an earlier statement, most individuals make financial decisions based on emotion and impulse rather than logic. Professional athletes lead this charge, and it explains why so many experience financial hardship in retirement. "Deserve" is one word that illustrates how deeply rooted this mindset can be. When an athlete believes they deserve something, they will find several emotional reasons to justify their rationale and support a decision they have already made. Remember when I asked you to create an unemotional process for making financial decisions? That process will help you avoid convincing yourself of what you deserve for your hard work.

As a professional athlete, you must transfer your discipline in your sport to your personal life and your financial situation. You must create a system to reward yourself, and you must keep the reward options practical. For instance, buying a private jet for winning one game is not a viable reward option because you will take on a long-term commitment for a short-term milestone. You can afford it right now, but it isn't a good long-term investment. You should adjust the way you see the big picture so that this system will leave you feeling rewarded without putting you in a financial bind. Even after this milestone has passed, you will still have savings and investment goals to meet. Some athletes, like the NFL's Marshawn Lynch and the NBA's Shaquille O'Neal, have found great success by limiting their lifestyle and expenditures to fit within what they earn for endorsements and saving every dime of their contracts. Talk about discipline!

Some ideas for creating a system of milestones you can use to reward yourself can be anything from winning a championship to earning team or league honors. This type of system has a longer-term focus and forces you to maintain a high level of work ethic, professionalism, and consistency. However, this process sometimes puts pressure on you to splurge on an expensive or high-level reward because you trick yourself into believing the rarity of the achievement calls for it. On the contrary, even though your rewards are for larger milestones that occur less frequently, you must still limit the size of the reward. Remember, you must remain disciplined at all times.

Many athletes purchase a home as a reward to themselves and their families, but I typically advise against purchasing a home early in your career because so many things could go wrong and leave you stuck with a note you can no longer afford. Once your career is off the ground, you can explore your options to purchase a home in cash and for a reasonable sum for yourself or your parents. Keep in mind—the larger the residence, the more expensive the upkeep. Most times, players overlook the maintenance costs of a large home, such as taxes, insurance, utilities, landscaping, security systems, housekeeping, etc. If your parents are no longer working, these costs will ultimately fall to you, and you may struggle to keep them up in retirement.

As an active athlete, I suggest renting or leasing a nice apartment or condo. You will travel most of the year for games, appearances, and vacations, and it is usually a lot more cost-effective to rent or lease your living accommodations. At any point you can even be traded to another team, and the hassle of selling a home and relocating can be stressful. As you near the end of your career, you may explore purchasing a home in an area where you expect to settle, especially if you have a family. The past decade has seen the highest occurrence of foreclosures, evictions, and unsustainable living arrangements among professional athletes, and I suspect that the primary reason is that they commit to living beyond their means too early in their careers.

Athletes also commonly utilize cars to reward themselves for various reasons. Most of the time, professional athletes spend too much money on these depreciating assets, buying more cars than they can drive in a week! An important consideration in any car-buying decision is whether to buy or lease, a decision largely based on your lifestyle, needs, and preferences. The main advantages to leasing a vehicle is that your payments are generally lower and you can transition to a new car every two to three years because of the short contracts. However, your mileage is limited, and repairing damage is expensive because you don't own the car. It must be returned at the end of the lease.

Buying a car outright has advantages because you can make any changes to it and have no mileage restrictions. It is also less expensive if you plan to keep the car long-term. The drawbacks to purchasing a car are the higher down payments required and the potential trade-in hassles if you decide to trade it for a new car. If you decide to trade the car for a newer model, you may find yourself upside-down in your payments, owing more on the car than it's worth, because most of your early car payments go toward interest on the loan. Depending on the situation, each option could work for you, so make sure you do your research. Although things happen, try to stick to your original plan as best as you can as changes can be costly.

Another common reward is a luxury vacation for an athlete, his family, and his friends. There are inexpensive vacation options, so please do your research with a certified travel agent. Remember, if you make your decision based on where your veteran teammates travelled or the amenities offered, you are likely to pay more than you should for a similar experience. There are cruises, resorts, islands, and other popular vacation rental options that will allow you to celebrate without committing a large amount of your resources for a one-time experience. I advise my clients to set aside a small amount of their income throughout the year to help them budget for their off-season and vacation.

This gives you a ceiling to guide your decision and helps you account for unforeseen travel costs in the vacation experience. Vacation rentals are popular but are usually expensive to maintain year-round. Again, research, research, research, using logic rather than emotion!

 Determine how you can reward yourself for achieving your career and personal goals by creating a written list of predetermined reward options for career, league, and team milestones. Try to prevent making emotional, impulsive decisions to reward yourself for your hard work. Limit your rewards to high-level achievements, and avoid making long-term commitments for short-term milestones. In short, be disciplined and follow your system!

Chapter 13

Preparing for the Rookie Year

 How do I prepare for my rookie year to avoid common mistakes?

"Without self-discipline, success is impossible, period."

–Former NFL player and coach, Lou Holtz

-13-

As you prepare for your first professional opportunity, you can do several things to get off to a good start and get the most from your experience without accumulating a lot of debt. During pre-draft training and preparation, I suggest that you stay on your college campus to train. Using your college facilities and trainers will not only save you a lot of money, but you will also maintain access to great trainers. Sometimes agents will lure you to training facilities in large cities to entice you to sign with their agency. While the facilities are usually world-class, the environment is usually ripe for distractions, and you may have to repay some of the expenses.

Adonal Foyle, NBA veteran, offers profound advice for athletes considering borrowing money from their agents until the draft: Don't do it! In his book entitled *Winning the Money Game*, Foyle writes, "If you're borrowing money from an agent until November, you have already made your first rookie mistake, depending on how much the agent wants in interest." NBA players are drafted in June but do not receive their first salary payment until November. NFL players are drafted in April or May but receive their first check when the regular season begins in August. Many athletes want to get a head start on spending like a professional athlete, and they amass debt before they receive their first check. Make sure you know if you have to repay any advances or if you are being charged interest on your loan. If you must ask to find out the answers to these questions, that should be your first red flag about your agent's trustworthiness.

Do not make any long-term purchase commitments; wait until at least the first couple of seasons have passed. This will enable you to maintain your focus on your career and give you an opportunity to see the direction it will go without the financial pressure of repaying debt.

As previously discussed, you will need to secure living accommodations, and I suggest renting or leasing an apartment or condo during your first few years as a professional athlete for several reasons, due to travel, cost effectiveness, and flexibility.

In general, I recommend that you rent or lease assets that drive, float, or fly. These vehicles, boats, and planes are all depreciating assets (assets that experience a gradual decline in value over time due to age, wear, and market conditions) with expensive price tags. Although your payment remains the same, if you lease, you are able to break the contractual agreement rather than be locked into paying for something that is continually and quickly losing value. These types of assets lose value as soon as you remove it from the seller's lot.

With the help of a financial professional, you should establish a budget of expenses for your first year as a professional athlete. If you take the time to create a budget, you must put forth great effort to stick to it for it to be effective. You must review your actual expenditures to determine if you met your goals or if adjustments are necessary. Otherwise, you run the risk of allowing emotional, impulsive decisions to dictate your financial start. Utilize less emotion and more discipline.

It will be tempting to emulate the things you see veterans do. Resist the urge to compete with their purchases, investments, and lifestyle choices. They usually have consistent income streams, residual endorsement earnings, and substantial savings that allow them to live more lavishly. If you retain a good veteran or retired mentor, these individuals can help you avoid mistakes that many rookies make. The NBA's Khawi Leonard still drives the same vehicle he drove in high school! Your ability to make sound decisions will be only as strong as the people you surround yourself with, so keep your circle small but full of wisdom.

You should make it a point to introduce yourself to your coaches, team personnel, and your players' association representatives when possible. This is a great networking opportunity in your market and throughout the league. Most of the executives and employees in your organization have worked in other organizations or have contacts in other areas of the league. You never know when that connection will be able to assist you with personal or professional issues.

Bullying and hazing for rookie athletes happens frequently. There are unspoken "rookie responsibilities" in each league and on each team. Some veterans make rookies carry all the pads after practice while others make rookies treat the entire team to dinner. Some of these activities are harmless and are part of the culture of initiating rookies to earn their acceptance into the sports family. However, there are times that the requests are taken out of context, and veterans use intimidation, bullying, and even hazing for personal pleasure. Although you may feel pressure to go along with certain things to be accepted, you should never compromise your self-respect, dignity, or safety to be a part of any team. Do not be afraid to speak up for yourself, and if the other team members continue destructive behavior, go speak to a coach or member of management. If these incidences continue, the negative effects on the team chemistry will be evident on the field or court anyway. You always have the power to teach people how to treat you, and you do that by making clear what you will and will not accept.

 You can do several things to make your first professional season a success. Perform pre-draft training on your college campus, never borrow money from your agent, rent or lease your living accommodations, rent or lease all depreciating assets, create and stick to your budget, avoid imitating veteran athletes' spending, and introduce yourself to your team executives for networking opportunities. Make sure you respond to any bullying or hazing quickly and appropriately.

Chapter 14

Using Digital Media Wisely

 How important is my social-media presence?

"As a professional athlete a lot is going to be said about you—but I just try to move forward and try to achieve my goals."

–NBA champion, LeBron James

-14-

As technological advances increasingly push us all to build our digital presence, the sports world has seen a shift in the way it promotes, connects, and interacts with its fan base. The rise of smartphones has given athletes a wealth of tools to connect, in real time, with their fans, the media, and their sponsors. There are applications on phones that enable athletes to share intimate photos, live videos, and Photoshopped images with the public that better illustrate their true interests, desires, and perspectives. Because of its global reach, influence on public opinion, and persuasive power, the digital space will increasingly become a vital branding and marketing tool for prominent sports figures.

As you continue to rely on digital platforms, like social media, to share snippets of your life with others, many decision makers will use your online presence to evaluate you for college scholarships, professional contracts, and even marketing opportunities. They can go back as far as your childhood and grade-school days to evaluate you. Your language, online activities, and preferred content give strong clues to your character and your values. The decision makers will use this information to determine if you would be a good fit for their program, team, or an open position. Duke University athletic scouts recently tweeted about ending a recruiting relationship with a prospect because of his social-media content. Understand that everyone is watching you, even NOW. And your online presence affects everyone you are associated with.

One important thing you should always remember when posting and tweeting is that once something enters the digital world, it is out there forever. Even after you delete it, it can be recovered. Individuals utilize a screenshot tool, taking an image of your post and saving it to their mobile device as a picture that can be recirculated at any time. Larry Nance Jr. was chosen in the 2015 NBA draft, and moments after his name was called, a tweet about Kobe Bryant's prior rape allegation that he sent out as a high schooler was recirculated. Nance was mortified and publicly acknowledged his embarrassment about his immature tweet. He later apologized to Bryant for joking about such an unfortunate moment for Bryant's family.

Although you can connect privately with other users on social media through direct messages that the public cannot see, nothing on social media is truly "private." Many users have used the screenshot tool to publicly humiliate other prominent figures and will sell their evidence to news outlets and blogs for a few moments of fame. I implore you to use your accounts wisely and never make the mistake of thinking anything is private or untraceable on any digital platform.

Facebook, Twitter, Instagram, and Snapchat are the most commonly used social-media platforms and can be used for a variety of strategic purposes. These platforms are important tools to create a coordinated marketing strategy about an athlete's brand. Because the tweets and posts are controlled by the athlete, they appear more authentic and genuine than other advertising methods. All sports fans want the opportunity to connect with the athlete as a person, not just as a public figure, so they follow their online activity for insight into their meals, preparation, and lifestyle. Publicists also use social media to quickly handle a professional athlete's crisis. For instance, sending out an apology or official statement through social media is a great way to respond quickly to a large group of people. Sponsors will even pay athletes a lot of money to tweet or post about the company's goods or services in hopes of persuading the athlete's fan base to make a purchase.

Awaiting his first-round NFL draft selection, Laremy Tunsil of the Ole Miss Rebels experienced the negative effects of social media's power. His Twitter and Instagram accounts were allegedly hacked. Leaked messages indicated that he illegally took money from his college coaches to pay his parents' bills, and videos showed him smoking from a bong. The negative effects of this blunder cost him millions of dollars as he dropped ten spots on the draft chart.

The NFL's Greg Jennings is one athlete that understands the power of using his social media for marketing purposes. He used his social-media account to interact with his fans while on pace to reach 500 career receptions. When he had 499 receptions, he hosted a Twitter contest for his fans to win a pair of his 500th reception game-worn gloves by guessing how many yards his 500th reception would be. He used a hashtag and drove traffic to his account. He even became a top-ten trending topic in the US!

When used appropriately, social media can be an effective marketing tool to increase fan engagement, manage a crisis, and secure sponsor dollars. Use the following guidelines to maximize your social-media presence:

- Establish a goal for each social-media account to guide the type of posts you share.

- Show your personality in your posts and tweets with humor, emojis, and abbreviations.

- Remember, everyone can see it (even your MOM!), and it can be recovered at any time.

- Do not speak negatively about another player, your team, or organization. It can hurt your career.

- Share your achievements and sports performances.

- Do not use profanity or explicit language.

- Be honest at all times. Lying creates a public firestorm.

- Post regularly, and fact-check any posts before sharing and commenting.

- Never post personal information like phone numbers, Social Security numbers, or account numbers.

- Always respond to your fans! They will be your biggest supporters during the lows of your career, and you don't want to establish an arrogant personality.

Remember, what you post now will affect you later, so always share appropriate content. Never assume that any private messaging is private. Your social media is used to assess your character and can be used to grow your brand. Practice using your social media to create your brand by sharing family moments, training sessions, meals, and hobbies. Always encourage your fans to interact with you by asking questions, holding contests, and spreading awareness for worthy causes.

Chapter 15

Utilizing the Resources of the Players' Association

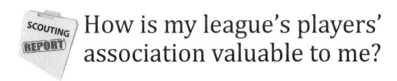 How is my league's players' association valuable to me?

"Stay focused.
Your start doesn't determine
how you're going to finish."

–Former NFL coach, Herm Edwards

-15-

I think all professional athletes should join and utilize the tresources of their league's player association. The organizations exist to protect and assist athletes with many important issues. The National Basketball Players' Association (NBPA) is the union for active NBA players. It was formed in 1954 to protect the rights of NBA players and to guide them to success in various areas on and off the court. According to their website, www.nbpa.com, the NBPA represents its players in many ways, such as:

- Negotiating the terms of a collective bargaining agreement with the NBA, which governs all aspects of players' employment

- Ensuring that the NBA and its teams meet their obligations under the CBA

- Certifying, regulating, and educating player agents

- Providing a full range of services, benefits, and assistance through the NBPA's Player Services department

- Monitoring and negotiating the administration of retirement and insurance benefits

- Providing on-staff security professionals to help with proprietary or sensitive matters

- Assisting charity and community organizations

- Promoting the positive image and reputation of NBA players, both on and off the court

Throughout the span of a player's career, there are a number of instances when the NBPA's services will prove necessary. Available to address player concerns seven days a week, 365 days a year, the NBPA is accessible to aggressively protect player rights and interests. Almost every player calls upon the NBPA at some point in his career to:

- Obtain expert legal advice and/or representation in a dispute

- Receive salary and pertinent information to assist in individual contract negotiations

- File a grievance

- Appeal a fine or suspension

- Help resolve player/agent disputes

- Protect medical benefits and other rights

There is also an association for retired NBA players. The National Basketball Retired Players Association (NBRPA) is a charitable 501(c)3 organization that seeks to help retired NBA, ABA, Harlem Globetrotters, and WNBA players in their post-career transitions. Additionally, the NBRPA works to positively impact communities and youth through basketball training and mentoring. The organization is supported by the NBA and NBPA and currently has over 700 retired professional athlete members.

Because an NBA athlete's average career spans just over four years, the need for long-term financial and health planning is critical. In 2016, the NBPA unanimously voted to fund health insurance for all retired players with at least three years of service in the league. This program is the first of its kind among professional sports organizations in North America. The board of directors and executive committee have vowed to focus on protecting the health and general welfare of current, retired, and future NBA players.

The NFL also has a union for its players called the National Football League Players' Association (NFLPA). Established in 1956, the NFLPA has a long history of assuring proper recognition and representation of players' interests. The NFLPA has shown that it will do whatever is necessary to assure that the rights of players are protected—including ceasing to be a union, if necessary, as it did in 1989. In 1993, the NFLPA again was officially recognized as the union representing the players and negotiated a landmark collective bargaining agreement with the NFL. The current CBA will govern the sport through 2020. It:

- Represents all players in matters concerning wages, hours, and working conditions and protects their rights as professional football players

- Assures that the terms of the collective bargaining agreement are met

- Negotiates and monitors retirement and insurance benefits

- Provides other member services and activities

- Provides assistance to charitable and community organizations

- Enhances and defends the image of players and their profession on and off the field

The NFL has a program that the NBA does not yet have to help protect its players from fraudulent management practices. While belonging to the NFL Players Association Advisor Program is voluntary for financial advisors, it is mandatory for contract advisors (a.k.a. agents). All NFL agents are fully regulated by the NFLPA and cannot conduct business without NFLPA certification and approval. Under regulations governing contract advisors, every agent may refer their clients only to financial advisors registered in the program; doing otherwise risks disciplinary sanction. Similarly, any agent providing financial advice must also be dually registered in the Financial Advisor Registration Program.

One important disclaimer worth mentioning is that the NFLPA doesn't endorse any advisor on its approved list. The list simply certifies that the advisor has passed a background check, is actively licensed, has been in business longer than eight years, and carries the appropriate professional liability insurance. Some NFL players have experienced fraud and misappropriation of funds by working with advisors on the approved list. It is important for you to understand that, while the NFLPA encourages you to work with advisors on their approved list, they hold no liability or responsibility for any loss, fraud, or misappropriation. You are, in fact, open to work with any financial professional of your choosing.

Per the NFLPA website, www.nflpa.com:

> *The NFLPA is not endorsing any Registered Player Financial Advisor, and is not responsible for, and disclaims, any liability for the acts or omissions of any Registered Player Financial Advisor. The NFLPA is also not responsible for, and makes no representation concerning, the skill, honesty, or competence of any Registered Player Financial Advisor, or any other person. The NFLPA is not in a position to determine whether Applicants for Registration as Registered Player Financial Advisors that provide Broker-Dealer, Investment Adviser, insurance sales, or other regulated financial services are properly registered with, licensed by, or otherwise in compliance with all rules and regulations of the appropriate federal and/or state governmental, or semi-governmental agency, authority, or organization. As a result, the NFLPA will rely entirely on the truthfulness of statements by any person or entity applying*

for Registration as an NFLPA Registered Player Financial Advisor that it has the necessary Broker Dealer, or Investment Adviser registration under applicable securities or commodities laws, SRO membership, licensing or other qualifications imposed by applicable federal and/or state law to render the financial services specified in the Application. Applicants will only be registered with respect to services disclosed in the Application.

I want to reiterate that you *do not have to work with a financial advisor on the* NFLPA's *financial advisor list!* You agent is required to recommend that you do, but the decision of who to work with is up to you. Remember, if someone on that list commits fraud or misappropriates your money, the league holds no liability for their crime. NONE! Former NFL players Vernon Davis and Fred Taylor recently opened up about their decision to work with an advisor on the approved list. Both men felt that they were making a good choice because of the advisor's registration with the NFLPA. This advisor lost a total of $43 million invested by several NFL players.

These scenarios happen often, and because they do not make the NFL look good, they aren't discussed publicly. Unfortunately, the NFL or NFLPA is not responsible for reimbursing the players. Learn the rules, read the fine print, and make the best decision for YOU!

The NFLPA also has resources for its retired athletes, and benefits to former players include assistance with joint replacement, Medicare supplements, vested life insurance, neurological care, spinal care, prescription drug cards, and assisted living resources. There are other organizations for former professional football players that help them network, stay connected to other former players, prepare for business opportunities, promote community involvement, and provide educational opportunities for long-term medical care. Do your homework to determine how these resources can be helpful to you and how you can help other athletes once you retire.

Understand the resources available to you through the NBPA and NFLPA. They have resources to protect you during your career and guide you through your post-career transition.

Scouting Report Summary

The recurring theme of this book is to encourage you to take responsibility for EDUCATING YOURSELF through the many resources available to you and to do the work required to protect yourself, your career, your reputation, and your legacy. In light of that theme, I have included some books for you to read to broaden your horizons and build a solid foundation to prepare for what you will face as a professional athlete. Remember, you must never cease learning, and what better way to learn than to learn from others? Your preparation now can assure your success later. Enjoy!

Scouting Report: How can I start building my legacy?

GAME PLAN: Ask yourself how you want to be remembered as a person, not just as an athlete. Imagine what you'd like people to say about you at your funeral. Make a list of those traits and the things you must do to be remembered that way. Most of your list should encompass how you treat and help others, not what you do for yourself. Start checking off your action items TODAY!

Scouting Report: How do I avoid the pre-fame leeches and handlers?

GAME PLAN: Make a list of anyone that is close to you outside of your parents, and write down how you met them. Be cautious about any person that you didn't meet naturally and that seems too eager to help. If it seems too good to be true, it usually is. Even if you've accepted aggressive advances in the past, you can always politely decline their advances moving forward. Don't risk your future on short-term pleasure.

Scouting Report: How do I build my own team of professionals and supporters?

GAME PLAN: Don't let your overconfidence in your ability to work with certain people cost you your family, your career, and your future. Don't be too trusting with one individual, no matter how well you get along. Leave the business to the professionals. Make a list of the qualified professionals in your family and close circle. Include at least one professional mentor that you have not yet met, but to whom you need to introduce yourself. Review your team often to make sure every member is accommodating your needs, and do not be afraid to make the necessary adjustments.

Scouting Report: How can I avoid ruining my family relationships?

GAME PLAN: It is never too late to make better decisions! Learn to share ideas and experiences instead of dollars and cents. When you change your mind-set, your relationships will change, but they will be more valuable. Create connections that will remain the same when money is removed from the conversation. Create a calendar of events for the next twelve months that includes quality family experiences without a financial focus. Make sure you have someone in place that can say "NO" for you to your closest family members and friends.

Scouting Report: How can I protect my mental health?

GAME PLAN: Talk to a mental health professional outside your school or team if you suspect you are having trouble dealing with certain feelings. Remember, mental health professionals are bound by confidentiality codes. Eliminate fear from your decision and put your overall health first. The sooner you address a mental illness issue, the healthier you will be. Utilize the treatment course recommended for you to avoid any lapses or setbacks.

Scouting Report: How should I take care of my body for long-term health?

GAME PLAN: You must do the work required to take care of your body for peak performance, career longevity, and quality of life. This includes following a healthy diet, sustainable training programs, and appropriate injury rehabilitation programs. Resist the urge to take shortcuts with performance-enhancing drugs and illegal substances as these substances will not only violate league drug policies, they also have the potential to become addictive and harmful to your long-term health. If you are injured, get your treatment plan in writing from a certified medical professional, and take the time you need to heal. Study the effects of CTE, and take any head injury very seriously.

Scouting Report: How do I avoid problems with the opposite sex?

GAME PLAN: Revisit the list you created about your legacy. If you did not include child-support issues, cheating scandals, promiscuity, or domestic-violence arrests, take every step you can to prevent those vices from ruining your life and your career. Visualize your reaction if your private text messages, conversations, and activities were made public. Be honest in your communication with those of the opposite sex, and take great care to remove yourself from potentially compromising situations. Remove family and friends from your circle that put you in positions to compromise your character.

Scouting Report: How important is cash flow to my financial security?

GAME PLAN: Learn about basic financial concepts, such as net worth, cash flow, and budgeting, to make strong short-term and long-term financial decisions. Understand how taxes and contract guarantees impact your take-home pay and contract longevity. Perform financial assessments regularly (at least monthly), and make the necessary adjustments to keep yourself on track for your goals. Do not make a long-term decision based on short-term income!

Scouting Report: How do I make better financial decisions to avoid hardship?

GAME PLAN: Hire a competent, trustworthy advisor and review with them often. Write out your financial goals and plans to achieve them. Break down your activities, budget by the week, and measure your progress. Make sure to secure life and disability coverage as soon as possible, and contribute regularly to a retirement savings plan. Make real-estate and other risky investments with only a small percentage of your income and only after you've educated yourself and evaluated the pros and cons.

Scouting Report: How can I maintain good credit? Why should I?

GAME PLAN: Understand how your credit is used to evaluate your character and your financial health, and use it wisely. Take the necessary precautions to safeguard your personal information and financial instruments against theft and fraud, and check your credit regularly to stay abreast of changes to your report. Check your report annually, and sign up for a monthly credit-monitoring service. Be careful about opening new credit cards if you can't afford to pay off what you charge each month. One mistake can take years to correct, so be proactive about protecting your credit rating as early as your college years!

Scouting Report: How do I begin preparing for what I will do when I retire?

GAME PLAN: Make a list of three alternative career paths for you outside sports and the qualifications needed for each. Make a plan, complete with a timetable, to finish your degree requirements. Find a mentor in your sport who can give you useful advice and who will push you to make good decisions. Utilize real-estate opportunities wisely, and always use the resources of your league's players' association.

Scouting Report: How can I save money but also enjoy some of the fruit of my labor?

GAME PLAN: Determine how you can reward yourself for achieving your career and personal goals by creating a written list of predetermined reward options for career, league, and team milestones. Try to prevent making emotional, impulsive decisions to reward yourself for your hard work. Limit your rewards to high-level achievements, and avoid making long-term commitments for short-term milestones. In short, be disciplined and follow your system!

Scouting Report: How do I prepare for my rookie year to avoid common mistakes?

GAME PLAN: You can do several things to make your first professional season a success. Perform pre-draft training on your college campus, never borrow money from your agent, rent or lease your living accommodations, rent or lease all depreciating assets, create and stick to your budget, avoid imitating veteran athletes' spending, and introduce yourself to your team executives for networking opportunities. Make sure you respond to any bullying or hazing quickly and appropriately.

Scouting Report: How important is my social-media presence?

GAME PLAN: Remember, what you post now will affect you later, so always share appropriate content. Never assume that any private messaging is private. Your social media is used to assess your character and can be used to grow your brand. Practice using your social media to create your brand by sharing family moments, training sessions, meals, and hobbies. Always encourage your fans to interact with you by asking questions, holding contests, and spreading awareness for worthy causes.

Scouting Report: How is my league's players' association valuable to me?

GAME PLAN: Understand the resources available to you through the NBPA and NFLPA. They have resources to protect you during your career and guide you through your post-career transition.

Acknowledgements

Thank you to my husband, for being one of my biggest supporters, my sounding board, and my voice of reason.

Thank you to my baby sister, Tandra, for being my loudest cheerleader and brainstorming partner.

Thank you to my Mama and my Daddy, for your smiles, your hugs, your encouragement, and unconditional love. I will spend my life trying to repay you.

Thank you to Terrance Metcalf, for sharing your journey with me and for confirming my calling.

Thank you to Yolanda Moore, for your fire, your confidence, and sharing your blueprint with me.

Thank you to my Lord, for your love, your mercy, your saving grace, and the vision to change lives.

Thank you to Crescendo Publishing, for believing in my vision and giving it life through your visual artistry.

About the Author - Tywanna Smith

Tywanna Smith, president and founder of The Athlete's NeXus, has several years of experience working with professional athletes in a financial and business capacity. Smith earned her bachelor of business administration (BBA) in marketing and her master of business administration (MBA) from The University of Mississippi (Ole Miss). She was also a four-year starter for the SEC program's women's basketball team, eventually taking her talents to Europe for a two-year professional career.

Upon retirement from professional athletics, Smith entered the corporate world with Merrill Lynch as a financial advisor to several professional athletes. In addition to handling her clients' finances, Smith has also managed the business and marketing affairs of several current and retired NBA, NFL, and overseas athletes. Over the past ten years, Smith has helped over a dozen professional athletes protect their assets, evaluate business opportunities, secure marketing endorsements, coordinate community-service events and appearances, start nonprofit organizations, and make significant life decisions. She has also connected her clients with reputable industry specialists, such as attorneys, accountants, real-estate specialists, travel agents, publicists, custom clothiers, and personal trainers.

Through a decade of work in the world of professional sports, Smith was led to create The Athlete's NeXus, A Sport Marketing & Business Management Group for NBA, NFL, and international athletes. She noticed the trend of financial hardship and negative stereotypes surrounding professional athletes and realized that many of them do not have quality professionals to help them navigate the opportunities and threats that come with being a public figure. This lack of preparation prevents a smooth transition to the next chapter of their lives. Her team manages every aspect of an athlete's lifestyle so that they can focus on their craft. They are committed to helping each professional athlete become a better citizen, a better role model, and a better businessman to positively impact the next generation of athletes.

Smith's husband, Jason, is a former international basketball player. They have one son together, Tyson.

I am a Woman of God, a Wife, a Mother, a Daughter, an Entrepreneur, an Author, and a Motivational Speaker.

I am great, because I believe it!

About The Athlete's Nexus

Founded in 2016, The Athlete's NeXus is a Sports Marketing & Business Management Solution for today's NBA, NFL, and international athletes. As a group of marketers, business managers, publicists, post-career counselors, and business consultants, we utilize a unique marketing and business management model to create value for our clients. Our model is twofold; we create customized, strategic PR and marketing plans for each client, which includes individual branding in each of their markets. We also manage business relationships between our clients and other professionals, such as accountants, trainers, and attorneys. Essentially, we manage all aspects of our clients' lives so that they can focus on their craft.

Our emphasis on individual branding, personal development, marketing opportunities, and post-career partnerships has helped our athletes build legacies that will positively impact the next sports generation. Our strategies are designed to help our clients develop their personal skill set to secure their post-career futures while they are actively playing. We conduct speech coaching, etiquette training, mentoring programs, networking opportunities, styling coaching, off-season branding, event planning, and PR initiatives.

Because most marketing and management firms focus on short-term revenue, many athletes fail to develop in areas that will help them transition smoothly and survive in retirement. We develop the athlete, personally and professionally, so that he is prepared to take advantage of any opportunity that is presented to him through his professional status. Our team is not driven by commissions; we are driven by results. We believe that it's about more than the game; it's about our clients' lives!

Connect with the Author

Websites:

www.theathletesnexus.com
www.survivingthelights.com

Email: contact@theathletesnexus.com

Address:

The Athlete's Nexus
1020 N. Gloster Street, Ste 169;
Tupelo, MS
38804

Social Media:

Facebook: https://www.facebook.com/TheAthletesNeXus/
LinkedIn: Tywanna Smith, MBA
Twitter: @AthletesNexus
Instagram: TheAthletesNexus

Resources

Carnegie, Dale. *How to Win Friends & Influence People*

Grover, Tim. *RELENTLESS: From Good to Great to Unstoppable*

Johnson, Spencer. *Who Moved My Cheese?*

Keller, Gary, Jenks, Dave, Papasan, Jay *The Millionaire Real Estate Investor*

Schoner, Bernd. *The Tech Entrepreneur's Survival Guide*

References

"Is the percentage of black NFL players going to reach NBA levels"? *quora.com*. https://www.quora.com/Is-the-percentage-of-black-NFL-players-going-to-reach-NBA-levels.

Bryant, Kobe. "Letter to My Younger Self." *theplayerstribune.com*. http://www.theplayerstribune.com/kobe-bryant-letter-to-my-younger-self.

CBC Sports. "O'Neal graduates from LSU." *cbcsports*. Dec. 15, 2000. http://www.cbc.ca/sports/basketball/o-neal-graduates-from-lsu-1.236228.

Conway, Tyler. "Antonio Cromartie's Estimated Child Support Revealed in NY Post Report." *bleacherreport. com*. Jan. 18, 2016. http://bleacherreport.com/articles/2608852-antonio-cromarties-estimated-child-support-reportedly-revealed.

Elliott, Bud. "Why Rivals.com has recruiting profiles for sixth graders now." *sbnation.com*. Feb. 17, 2015. http://www.sbnation.com/college-football-recruiting/2015/2/17/8047771/rivals-middle-school-football-recruiting.

Espn.com. "Darren McFadden claims ex-financial planner mishandled $15M." *espn.com*. http://www.espn.com/nfl/story/_/id/16072610/darren-mcfadden-dallas-cowboys-sues-former-business-manager-15-million.

Foyle, Adonal. *Winning the Money Game*. New York: HarperCollins, 2015.

Gulliver, Amelia, et al. "The mental health of Australian elite athletes." *Journal of Science and Medicine in Sport* 18, no. 3. (May 2015): 255-261. http://www.jsams.org/article/S1440-2440(14)00075-9/abstract?cc=y=).

Jones, Kimberly. "Randy Gregory: 'I blame myself' for failed NFL combine drug test." *nfl.com.* March 25, 2015. Updated March 26, 2015. http://www.nfl.com/news/story/0ap3000000481581/article/randy-gregory-i-blame-myself-for-failed-nfl-combine-drug-test.

Keown, Tim. "Financial requests overwhelm Smith." *espn.com.* Nov. 26, 2014. http://www.espn.com/nfl/story/_/page/hotread141125/dallas-cowboys-tyron-smith-gets-control-battling-family-money.

Legwold, Jeff. "NFL's substance abuse and performance-enhancing drugs policies." *The Denver Post.* July 22, 2013. Updated April 29, 2016. http://www.denverpost.com/2013/07/22/nfls-substance-abuse-and-performance-enhancing-drugs-policies.

NBPA. "About & History." *nbpa.com.* http://nbpa.com/about.

NBRPA. "About the NBRPA." *National Basketball Retired Players Association.* http://www.legendsofbasketball.com/who-we-are/about-the-nbrpa.

NFLPA. "About the NFLPA." *The NFL Players Association.* https://www.nflpa.com/about.

NFLPA. "Financial Advisors: Application and Renewal." *nflpa.com.* https://www.nflpa.com/financial-advisors/financial-advisors-application-and-renewal.

Okung, Russell. "Betting on Myself." *theplayerstribune. com.* July 20, 2015. http://www.theplayerstribune.com/ russell-okung-seahawks-agents-in-sports.

Paikert, Charles. "How to Fix the Industry's Race Problem." *Financial-Planning.com.* Aug. 4, 2014. http://www.financial-planning.com/news/how-to-fix-the-industrys-race-problem.

Ruoff, Justin. "NFL Players lost $43M off financial advice by registered NFLPA agent." *Pigskin.* Oct. 24, 2016. http://www.todayspigskin.com/pigskin-news/nfl-players-lost-43m-off-financial-advice-registered-nflpa-agent.

Smith, Michael David. "Phillip Buchanon's cautionary tale: My mom demanded $1 million." *profootballtalk. com.* April 11, 2015. http://profootballtalk.nbcsports. com/2015/04/11/phillip-buchanons-cautionary-tale-my-mom-demanded-1-million.

Made in the USA
Columbia, SC
20 July 2018